Gift Shop at the DMZ

A Therapist Travels with the Military

MAUREEN HICKS

DANCING TREES PRESS

979-8-9891896-0-1 Print
979-8-9891896-2-5 ebook

Book design by Asya Blue Design

Printed in the United States of America

Author's Note
I've changed the names of people in this book to respect privacy. The healthcare corporation's name is changed as well, and it didn't use the MRC name I've chosen for the therapist jobs in the book. What happened — and when and where — is completely accurate as I remember it.

May I be a guard for those who are protectorless,
A guide for those who journey on the road.
For those who wish to go across the water,
May I be a boat, a raft, a bridge.

—Shantideva
The Way of the Bodhisattva

CONTENTS

CHAPTER 1

THE CALL

2003-2008

At the weekly staff meeting for Adult Services in a basement room of the County Mental Health Agency, the fluorescent lights flicker and buzz overhead. The pot-bellied manager sits on a desk, swinging his legs as he speaks. "Starting tomorrow, I want to see everyone here by 8 a.m. sharp. That's just standard for the organization. There's no reason our department should be any different."

"Except we're not paid as hourly employees," I say, trying to keep my voice neutral. "We're professional staff." Two co-workers throw me half-smiles. They know where this is going. "If we stay late to finish up and come in a few minutes later the next day," I continue, "that would be *standard* for professional employees."

The manager grunts and gestures with his hand as if to wave a pesky gnat away from his walrus mustache.

I press on. "We're paid to do our job and I think we all do a good job. Why is this such a big deal?"

Here's the part I don't say aloud: I'm tired of this get-your-assin-your-chair-when-I-say-so bullshit. I've worked for fifteen years as a psychologist in various agencies, and this place is by far the worst. Management issues orders left and right for misguided new procedures and likes to talk about the "chain of command." No respect is shown to the workers, whose input and opinions are seen as irrelevant. A conservative good old boys' network dictates this county's policies. They don't even believe government should offer social services, but if they must, they want it "run like a business." Or maybe even like the Army.

He glares at me. "On-time arrival is a big deal to the management. They're negotiating right now for a time clock system."

"A time clock? Seriously?"

"Everyone's going to have to punch in. So get over it."

"That makes no sense."

"Lots of things make no sense to you, Maureen," he says, menace in his voice. "It's called being oppositional."

I feel myself flush as he slaps on this clinical label. By the time the meeting is over I am seething and something shifts in my core. This is my Last Straw. On the way out the door, I mutter to a friend, "Now I understand what it means to go postal. If I don't get out of this place soon, somebody is going to get hurt."

I need to leave before they find a way to fire me from this civil service job. I don't want to go into private practice and try to sell my services on the open market, but what choice do I have? I am not naturally an entrepreneur, but my self-respect is dwindling the longer I remain in this situation. I close my eyes and take the leap of resigning.

A few months after my last day at the County I have lunch in Yreka with a former co-worker, Gini, at a local hangout, an old diner that's been turned into a Chinese restaurant. "I saw your name on the door of an office down the block," she says as we slide into a booth. "So you're really doing it!"

She's seen the gold lettering I hired someone to stencil on the door's window, Maureen Hicks, Ph.D., Clinical Psychologist. A nice touch. "I'm getting started, anyway. I got a lease, bought some furniture, put an ad in the Yellow Pages. I'm trying to get on the schedule to talk at the Rotary Club. I keep saying, 'Build it and they will come.' Here, take one of my cards."

"Nice card," she says, turning it over and smiling to read on the reverse, Be Here Now. "How's the business going?"

"Oh, as well as could be expected. So far just a couple of clients." I try to arrange my face to project optimism.

"So why didn't you open your practice in Ashland, where they believe in psychotherapy? It's redneck country over here."

"I've worked six years in this county. I'm hoping I've got helpful connections here." I stir my Twice-Cooked Garlic Pork and lift a bite to my mouth, proudly demonstrating my competence with chopsticks. "Besides, there are already too many therapists in Ashland."

THE TRUTH IS, MY PRACTICE HAS HAD A SLOW START, but I expected that. I console myself that I can borrow from my retirement fund to tide me over for now. I enjoy the increase in free time and the luxury of pondering questions larger than what I studied in college or graduate school: the possibilities of human potential, the nature of healing, the meaning of life. I volunteer as a librarian in Ashland at the Rogue Valley Metaphysical Library, which has a vast collection of books and videos on extraterrestrial visitations, near-death experiences, and other paranormal phenomena.

Hundreds of books on Western philosophy, Eastern religions, energy medicine, astrology, shamanism, and other topics line the shelves. An entire world my Western scientific training taught me to ignore and even disparage.

One day, as I'm sitting at the check-out desk, a man comes in and returns two videos on crop circles. "Have you seen these?" he asks. "They're aerial views from airplanes over England, and all these amazing designs that someone has made. God knows who, or how." I take them home to watch, and I'm impressed with the beauty and precision of the different designs, clearly not something that a person or even a group could have stomped out in the dark field overnight. I can't say for sure whether it was done by extraterrestrials, but if not, then who? I allow myself to wonder and be amazed. I wander through the stacks and pick out spiritual biographies and books on Buddhism, long an interest of mine. This is a seeker's heaven. I secretly pretend I'm the Scholar-in-Residence, delving into the riches of the library.

Over the next four years , my psychotherapy practice struggles and sputters. Other therapists in town view me as an unwanted competitor, and send me no referrals. I take classes on "How to Market your Therapy Practice." I join the Yreka Rotary Club to make contacts, but I feel out of place in this group whose idea of charitable work is to buy new American flags for the city's school classrooms. I get a gig doing cognitive testing for clients of the welfare department. Medicare pays me a pittance, and corporate insurance connives not to pay at all and sends me into repetitive loops of phone calls and re-billing.

In February 2008, I prepare my taxes for the previous year. My income, never enough to pay all my bills, has actually gone down. The country has just stumbled into the Great Recession. People are broke, unemployed. Overwhelmed and feeling inadequate, I'm disintegrating into fear and panic. My savings are almost depleted. Oh, the shame of it! I have fleeting thoughts of suicide, though I wouldn't act on them. I try self-help techniques and desperately tap on my body reciting, "I completely love and accept myself even though my world is crashing."

I lie on my bed, thoughts swirling around. *What will you do now? You don't have any real, marketable skills. You've spent all your savings. You're a profligate, a wastrel.* I want someone to appear who will take care of me and support me, but no one does. I've been single since a break-up five years back, and unhappy with my status. I've learned to be my own best friend and to focus on the freedom of being single, but have never stopped scanning for a potential life partner. I'm sad this person has not turned up yet.

FORTUNATELY I HAVE MANY GOOD AND WISE FRIENDS. One encourages me to think of this as a dark night of the soul, a spiritual crisis. I have a long talk with another, who says, "This is an ordeal, but you'll get through it. There will be important lessons." A third says, "Your life is being disassembled. Enjoy the ride!" They all assure me that prayer and meditation will be the best medicine.

My ego is exhausted. I feel very done with something. Maybe its death must precede the new chapter. Even though I'm still going to the office, I start deep-cleaning my house, divesting myself of excess possessions. This feels right, to clean up my act. I'm taking down the illusion of professional success. The chemistry of my body starts to settle down.

Since my twenties I've read Buddhist books and practiced meditation for brief periods, always remaining a curious beginner. Recently I began to attend meetings with two American women ordained as lamas in the Tibetan tradition, who extend an invitation to participate in a ceremony called "Taking Refuge Vows." I love the sound of the word refuge right now, but I'm uncertain what to do.

"Can I take Refuge Vows even if I don't know what that means?" I ask Lama Pema.

She laughs. "Of course."

I go to the ceremony in March with a sense of wonder and surrender, and recite, "I take refuge in the Buddha, the *Dharma*, and the *Sangha*." I'm given a Tibetan name, Choyang Lhamo, which means, "Goddess of Melody." Oh, that is sweet. Now I belong to a community, a *sangha*, which meets to study *dharma*, or Buddhist teachings.

IN APRIL I GET A PHONE CALL FROM MY FRIEND Stephanie. She tells me about a chance to work with a massive corporation that I'll describe with an alias.

"I've got to tell you about this new job," she says. "It's through Malwell Health Corporation. They send you to military bases and you walk around and talk to people and the pay is really good."

"Military bases? I can't picture this."

"I just got back from a month at Fort Drum in New York."

"Doing what?"

"I saw a couple people for counseling, but I didn't have much to do and that was fine with me. I've told you I'm lazy, right?"

"You must be kidding. What's the catch?"

"There's no catch. Think gravy train. Some of the jobs are even overseas."

It seems too good to be true. A well-paid job in 2008 when no one is hiring, except apparently, the military. The job is touted as a "no records kept" service, with the idea that military people would be more likely to come for counseling if there is no paper trail they fear could jeopardize their job. As a Military Resiliency Coach (MRC) I'd be a contractor on short-term assignments, with minimal oversight. All that is required is any type of mental health license.

I develop a fantasy of having my heart opened to people I would ordinarily avoid. I already see myself meditating in my hotel room with a shelf of wonderful books to read, being a quiet, accessible presence. Traveling to interesting places. Paying my bills and socking away the money. First thing I'll need is a new laptop. I wonder where I can find an inflatable meditation cushion. I'm astonished at how I have no hesitation and seem to be jumping in feet first. That week I apply for the job and for a passport renewal.

THREE WEEKS LATER, THE PHONE RINGS. A woman's voice says, "So you're interested in the MRC job?

"Yes, I am. Will I be doing counseling as a coach?"

"Sometimes. Or you might do what we call 'walking social work,' where you meet people casually and see if you can be helpful."

Walking social work — is she joking? What school of social work teaches that random schmoozing with people is a professional activity? I tell her I'm interested in the job.

"Is there is any sort of special preparation you'd recommend to get ready for this job?" I ask, wondering about the possible issues of military personnel and veterans.

"Oh, you might want to look up the local currency and the exchange rate."

That's it? I was expecting a job interview. Am I getting involved in some sort of governmental boondoggle where money is spent to look good, not to make a difference? I don't care. I need money and want an adventure!

"Could you be ready to go to Germany in one month?"

It takes a moment to find my voice. "Sure, that would be fine."

I hang up and think, what have I just done? I have no experience with the military, and ever since the Vietnam War I've identified as anti-war and critical of the defense budget. Have I lost my mind? How could someone like me survive in such an alien environment? And how could the military allow such an unsuitable person into their midst? I don't know yet how this will work, but I'm going for it.

The next week, as we hike around Hyatt Lake in the mountains above my home in Oregon, my old friend Bets asks, "So what's this I hear about you working for the military?"

"Sounds crazy, huh? When Jill told me she was signing up, I thought — no *way* I could work for the military, no matter how much they paid me."

"What made you change your mind?"

I give her a guilty look. "How much they pay me. And — it sounded like an adventure."

"But aren't you the original antiwar protester? The hippie love child?"

"I've gone undercover. Hadn't you noticed? I'm a psychologist now. Very respectable."

"So you think you can maintain that cover in the military?"

"Why not? I'm not actually joining up. I'll be a contractor and just have to keep my act together for a few weeks at a time, maybe a couple of months."

"Well, I get it that you need money, but this is a surprise. I don't think I'd want to jump into that soup. Probably ultra-conservative." She stops walking and turns to me, raising her eyebrows. "They don't allow gays in the military, you know."

"It's not like I have a rainbow tattoo. It's nobody's business, anyhow."

We stop to sit on a rotting log shaded by tall cedars. "Actually," I say, "I'm surprised they let me have the job. But they're not going to ask me about my personal beliefs, so how would they know?"

"You'd better leave your Birkenstocks at home."

Three dear friends come to my house to give me a send-off blessing, burning sage and saying heartfelt prayers that I will be protected and find ways to do good wherever I go. My joyful final step is a trip to my old office where, with a razor blade, I slowly scrape the gold lettering off the glass of the front door.

CHAPTER 2

PIGLET JOINS THE ARMY

2008

I land in Frankfurt after a sleepless overnight flight from San Francisco. Collecting my bags and going through customs, I detect a strange energy around me. U.S. military personnel wear civilian clothes but their exceedingly short haircuts give them away. After getting my luggage into a large cart, I ferry it across a skybridge to the Sheraton Airport Hotel and check in as I've been instructed. I need my key card to unlock the elevator, traveling to the fifth floor with expressionless clean-shaven men in dark glasses. I have a sense of being in some kind of cloak-and-dagger movie where an ominous, soulless force holds sway. A persistent sound of drilling edges into my room, but where does it come from? The next room? The ceiling? I become convinced they're installing spy equipment, and I demand a room change. At the front desk they politely hand me a new key.

Friends have said that the best way to deal with jet lag is to stay awake until evening, then sleep. I turn on the television and promptly fall asleep in the chair. The sound of snoring wakes me up. My chin has fallen to my chest. A German voice is describing the opening ceremonies of the Beijing Summer Olympics. A man with a torch in one hand is riding a bicycle on a tightrope. I fall asleep again.

I give up watching television and go downstairs to one of this luxury hotel's several restaurants in search of supper. I order a bowl of soup and a bottle of water and get charged 20 Euros, too steep for my budget. I'm still hungry, so I decide to keep myself awake by exploring the five-level small city which is the Frankfurt airport. I dream my way through the brightly-lit corridors, past ticket counters and high-end shops selling clothing and luggage, passing people of all colors, many of whom have brought their dogs. In my sleep-deprived state I find myself wondering, Who am I? Why am I here? I don't seem to be at all clear on this. The spicy smell of sausage draws me to a stand where it's being cooked. Hot sausage and potato salad make a meal. Back in the hotel room, I go right to sleep.

The next morning, in a hotel conference room in the basement, a group of us gather for our orientation to the role of Military Resiliency Coach. Each of us is an MRC, which we learn is pronounced "Merk." Fifteen American mental health professionals sit quietly around a large table while a majestic, dark-skinned man addresses us, to the accompaniment of long beaded braids clicking at his back. He is the chief of European operations for the corporate giant which has negotiated a hefty contract with the Department of Defense. We are the deliverables. We are told that the purpose of our six-week assignments will be to provide residents of military bases an opportunity to talk confidentially with someone outside their community, a counselor who will disappear after six weeks and will not be encountered socially. Not keeping records of these conversations is expected to encourage participation by those who fear if they'd consult regular Army mental health services, it would somehow get back to their command. Most of us will be working with adults, but a few have been assigned to work in Army schools and daycare centers. At home we may have been independent practitioners, but the tall man makes it clear that in this job we are to think of ourselves as interchangeable parts in a big machine as we engage in our brief rotations.

In his commanding voice he informs us of our rules of engagement: Do as you're told by your Point of Contact, which he calls a POC. Everything in this military world has an acronym. The POC is typically an Army civilian at our base. Learn the Army acronyms in order to appear knowledgeable. Smile in a friendly way and offer to be of service to military personnel and their families. Don't question anything. Provide off-the-record counseling sessions to soldiers and family members who wish to discuss relationship issues. If you don't have any counseling appointments, walk about and engage people in conversations, find openings to do informal counseling , but above all—"stay in your lane."

Stay in your lane? I gather he means we must do as we're instructed and only as we're instructed. We are to take no initiative to expand the parameters of the job, and we must be scrupulous not to intrude on any other group's turf. Other groups of Army personnel are tasked with offering traditional psychiatric services, group therapy, suicide prevention programs, and spiritual counseling. We must not do any of these, or we risk being fired.

In the afternoon after the orientation, I repack my bags and find my way to the train station on the lowest level of the airport. I'm burdened with two suitcases and a daypack, as well as a large soft leather briefcase and my purse, both slung around my neck.

I'm trying to act as though I can manage this on my own. Kind German strangers help me get all this gear onto the train, and I collapse into a seat in a first-class carriage. The ride is fast and smooth and the windows are clean. Farms and fields fly by, where many of the picturesque houses in small villages have solar panels on the rooftops. I make a note that Germany seems to be ahead of the U.S. in environmental awareness. In Wurzburg I change to a slower local train and proceed to my destination.

"Welcome to Bamberg!" says Karen, extending her hand as I walk toward her on the train platform. "I'm the Merk for the children's program." Her taupe-colored slacks and crisp white sleeveless top have me guessing she's from New England, or perhaps the Midwest. Another middle-aged woman stands next to her on the train platform. This is Honey, who is large and blonde with blood-red lipstick, a loose canary-colored blouse flowing about her ample bust. Honey grins and says, "I'm new like you, just got here a week ago. I'm gonna be your partner working with the adults."

Jet-lagged and disheveled, I mumble my thanks and let Karen help me get my bags into her black compact rental car. It's my second day in the country and I'm exhausted. Honey is limping and I ask her about it.

"Oh, yeah. I twisted my ankle rushing to catch my plane. I can't walk very far now, and it hurts."

Inside the car, Honey asks with that same wide grin, "Where're you from?"

"Oregon."

"Oregon," she drawls in three slow syllables. "Well, bless your heart! I'm from Arkansas."

"Ah, I've never been there."

"Well, I don't spend too much time there myself these days. My stuff is in storage because I'm traveling so much with this job."

"But what about when you're between assignments?"

"Oh, I'll stay with my parents, or with girlfriends. I tell people I'm homeless," she says with a giggle.

Karen's buttoned-down attire belies the inner wildness that comes out at the wheel as she races through the narrow streets of this old German town to the Hertz rental office. She screeches into the driveway and comes to a halt in a small lot full of cars. "Here's where you pick up your car. We'll wait so you can follow us to the hotel."

Inside the office, I sign for the car and they hand me keys to another black compact. I cross the parking lot and knock on the window of Karen's car. When she rolls it down, I say, "Go slow." She looks puzzled. "I don't want to lose you. I can't understand the signs and I don't have a map."

"Roger that." She and Honey jounce out the driveway and into the street, pausing briefly to make sure I'm behind. In five minutes we arrive at a four-story building with shops on the ground floor and offices above. We drive into the underground parking lot and take an elevator to the third floor, where the dozen or so rooms of a small hotel are tucked. I check in and dump my bags in a neat, modest room with two single beds, a desk, a chair, and a tiny bathroom. Then Karen says, "Now we have to get you your base ID." We all pile into her car, and she careens off to a small office a few blocks away, where once I show my passport and my contract, I am photographed and handed the card that will allow me to enter the U.S. Army installation.

We proceed to the base, which is nearby within the city limits.

Karen slows suddenly to navigate through a maze of concrete barriers. We come to a stop in front of an imposing two-story gatehouse. Guards peer down from the glassed-in watchtower above us, holding automatic weapons. German nationals inspect our documents and use a long-handled mirror to check under the car chassis for explosives.

Inside the gate is an old German garrison with cobblestone streets and walkways. As we cross over an unused railroad track, I get a chill thinking of the German trains that took so many to their deaths when these buildings were new. Now the old stone barracks buildings have been stuccoed and repainted in pastel colors, and Karen explains these are now offices and living quarters for American soldiers and family members. It almost feels like a small college campus, with grassy lawns, a large natural pond, and a new multimillion-dollar Freedom Fitness Facility. To my complete surprise, there is also a Burger King, a Subway, and a Popeye's, giving off the smell of hot grease.

Honey asks to be let off at her car, which she'd left in front of the DFAC (Dining Facility) before they came to pick me up. As she gets into the car I notice the seats and floors are covered with used coffee cups, candy wrappers, and other refuse. She rolls down her window. "I know we're going to get along fine. You know how some people are a Type A personality? Well, I'm so laid back, I say I'm a type D!" She explodes with laughter at her joke.

"Yeah, sure." I'm not sure at all, but I push out a smile.

THE NEXT MORNING HONEY AND I MEET with Jane, the designated Merk liaison. Here come more acronyms. Jane is a civilian worker with ACS (Army Community Services). She's a little dynamo, the petite and feisty wife of an NCO (non-commissioned officer). She takes each new set of arriving Merks on a tour of the facilities and introduces us to the important players in this community of less than two thousand people, such as the school principal and the base commander. She shows us an office we'll be using and the desk we'll be sharing. Honey promptly spills her coffee all over it.

"I'm so glad you Merks are here," Jane says. "The soldiers can really use some of your off-the-record counseling." She's devoted to her job promoting the well-being of Army families, offering classes in Army Family Team Building (AFTB). In these classes she tries to interest soldiers' spouses in learning how the Army works so that they know their rights and can claim their benefits, and not have to rely on their soldier spouse to decode mysteries like base assignment, deployment, promotion, and other protocol. She has scheduled me and Honey to do a presentation next week for the spouses of soldiers who are expected to return soon from a combat area. Our task is to help prepare spouses for the issues that often arise when soldiers return to the family and community after the hardship of separation and combat. Malwell has provided us with dozens of canned PowerPoint presentations that we are allowed to choose from to suit the occasion. We are not permitted to use our own initiative beyond ad-libbing each bullet point. Honey and I choose one we will do together, and I start thinking about what I might say.

THE FIRST WEEK BRINGS NO CALLS REQUESTING counseling, so I wander about the base admiring the lush green lawns and cobblestone walkways. The walk begins to get me used to being surrounded by people wearing rumply camouflage outfits and maroon berets. In Frankfurt they told us that often we'd be obliged to serve in a casual, stealthy way — showing up as friendly, available, trustworthy, and wise. We're apparently supposed to come alongside people, engage them in conversation, draw them out, get them to talk about their lives, what the corporation calls "walking social work," a term I'd never heard in my entire career. I cannot imagine such encounters being more than superficial, and as an introvert, such behavior feels unnatural. I imagine that strangers might not like to be buttonholed in this way. On my walks I mostly just smile and nod and leave people alone.

My own world-view is liberal and anti-authoritarian and that is clearly not the norm here, where authority comes from the top down through the chain of command and everyone is supposed to know their place. It's as though I've been dropped behind enemy lines, inserted as some sort of parasite, albeit a friendly one. I must conceal my political beliefs and liberal attitudes, so I worry about being unmasked. Someone has already given me a curious look and asked, "Did you used to be a hippie?" The remark was a friendly one, but it makes me worry — is it my comfortable shoes? My hair? Does my lack of makeup give me away?

Here I am, surrounded by soldiers who are typically assigned to German bases for three years. Their families bring tons of household goods and personal vehicles, at unimaginable expense to U.S. taxpayers. Observing this unfamiliar subculture, learning its language and assumptions, taking notes and photographs, I feel like a spy, or perhaps an anthropologist. I don't belong here, so I keep my head down and try to blend in as best I can. But I am fascinated by this opportunity to study a different culture at close range.

I START MODESTLY. MY FIRST OUTREACH ATTEMPT is to seek out the Base Chaplain in his office. I imagine the Merk's task is similar to that of the chaplains — inserting oneself into another's life in order to offer support. I'm hoping the two of us might have things in common and even want to work together to serve soldiers' emotional needs. He only has time for a brief chat, but on the way out the door says, "Come to the chapel service!" I'm not sure what to expect, but he seems so pleasant I decide to go on Sunday.

I slip into a pew near the back, and join in when it's time to sing a hymn or recite a prayer. Then the young sandy-haired chaplain launches into his sermon. He's only been speaking a few minutes when he starts to choke back tears. "God loves you! And He wants to forgive you! Oh, God loves you so much! Jesus wants to walk with us and He shows us the way, the way to be in harmony with God's commandments, to be saved from sin. To dwell with Him forever in His holy kingdom."

And here he almost starts to sob. "When I think that any of my brothers and sisters might continue in their heedless ways and fail to accept the Lord, it breaks my heart. Some of us are about to leave for Iraq, a dangerous place. If some lose their lives without having accepted Jesus as Savior — what then? How can we meet in Heaven if we have turned away from God in order to satisfy our lust, our cravings, our empty pleasures?"

He pauses to steady himself, then continues in this vein, but I'm not listening anymore. My heart aches to witness his visible anguish. His God is stern and punitive, and withholds heaven from people forever if they don't comply with the rules. This sweet, vulnerable chaplain is convinced that an Almighty king with only conditional love governs the universe. Rather than preaching the joy and peace inherent in practicing compassion and love for one's neighbor, the chaplain focuses on how breaking the rules leads to eternal punishment.

I walk out into the hazy sunshine of a summer's morning, shaken and perplexed. I come from a Christian background, but a liberal one where there were no hellfire and damnation sermons, just Jesus as a model of loving kindness. In a similar way, my understanding of Buddhism is that judgment prevents clear seeing of ourselves and others, and that an open heart and compassionate attitude are fundamental to leading a good life. How do I make common cause with someone whose passionate mission is to save souls for Jesus by frightening them into compliance?

One afternoon, Honey and I are asked to staff a newcomers event. We stand side by side behind a card table with our brochures and business cards. As a line of soldiers new to the base files by a series of such tables, we try to snag them long enough to pitch our program and hand them a brochure. Honey is better at capturing their attention than I am. As I straighten out the piles of brochures, I overhear her say, "So if you fellas need anything, we're your girls!" *Girls? I sure as hell am not anybody's girl.* I glower at her, but she pays no attention, reaching for the soldiers' hands and thanking them for their service. I'm floored, and can't think of a thing to say.

Honey likes to have lunch early, so I tend to say I'm going for a walk, and then come back to the DFAC later when she's gone. Her noisy "Type D" personality jangles my nerves. The food at the DFAC is surprisingly good, and it is comforting to be fed by the soldiers and the German cafeteria ladies. I develop the habit of eating a big hot lunch and then snacking in my room at suppertime on cold cuts, crackers, cheese, and German white wine.

"I'll have the barbecued ribs, please. Two. No, three … and some greens … and a little of the beans. Oh, cornbread — yes definitely." I make my way slowly along the cafeteria line, encouraging the servers to heap my plate. It's Soul Food Thursday at the DFAC, and my mouth is watering. I help myself to a glass of iced tea and look around the low-ceilinged dining hall to see where I might eat my lunch. Across the room I recognize a lean, wiry dark-skinned man eating and chatting with another community services worker and a couple of soldiers. As I approach their table, he gestures for me to join them.

"Hey, Maureen — how's it going?"

"Hey, Henry. Pretty well, I guess." I settle into a seat across from him. "You know, the Army is new to me, so I have a lot to learn."

He laughs. "Well, feel free to ask me anything you want to know. I was a soldier for twenty years, retired as a First Sergeant."

I'm so new I don't even know what a First Sergeant is, but I don't let on. "How did you like being in the Army all that time?"

"Oh, it was a great ride. I'm from Haiti, you know. I joined the U.S. Army when I was 18, after my parents died. The Army gave me an education, trained me, and sent me all over the world. But I liked Germany the most, so now I get to work here as a civilian." I like his way of speaking. No accent, really, but he pronounces his words more precisely than most Americans.

"Have you ever been back to Haiti?"

His face clouds a little while he hesitates. "No. I sort of lost touch with my family. They used to just get in touch when they wanted me to send money..."

Maybe I shouldn't pursue that over lunch. Clearly a painful subject. But I am curious and would like to know him better. I've noticed that soldiers tend not to volunteer opinions about the wars they're involved in, but I wonder if a civilian might be willing to talk more. I decide to ask him, "Did you ever go *downrange*?" I use this word with secret pride. I've heard soldiers use it to mean they got sent to a war zone.

"Not really. I watched the Gulf War on television, and it was over before they had a chance to mobilize my unit at Fort Hood. I retired in 2000, before 9/11 happened."

"Is that a good thing, or do you wish you could have gone?"

"Hmmm," he muses, chewing his food. "Honestly?" He looks around quickly to see if we can be heard in the din of the dining hall. "From what I hear, it's been pretty frustrating over there. You don't know where the enemy is hiding, and you don't know which civilians can be trusted and which are in cahoots with the Taliban. Or Al Qaeda. Or whoever it is we're fighting." He stops, maybe thinking he's said too much.

"Well, what do you think will happen? Can we do any good over there?"

"The way I look at it is this: Either we stay, and things get worse, or we leave, and things get worse."

I nod. He's just captured my own sense of the futility of the U.S. presence in Iraq and Afghanistan. I hesitate to pursue this potentially political subject. I don't want to set anybody off, but it's too late. His friend seated across from us has been listening, and shakes his head. He's a Black man in his sixties, also ex-military. "We really need to go in there and finish the fight," he says firmly. "Those Muslims have to be defeated. You know, we live in a Christian country. And they want to come here and take over, make everyone believe like them!"

I'm taken aback. Conservatives often aver that "America is a Christian country," yet this man's proudly stated belief that Muslims intend to take over America was going a step further than I'd heard before. I decide it's best not to try to respond. I take a big bite of the ribs and say again how good they are. Henry seems to welcome a change of subject, and agrees heartily. "These folks really do know how to do ribs!"

THE DAY OF OUR SCHEDULED PRESENTATION for the spouses arrives. Jane has put out publicity and hopes for a good showing. No one comes. We sit around and talk with her and other ACS staff about why this might have happened.

"It's not that surprising when you think about it," says Jane. "The last group of soldiers went on a tear when they got home."

"Yeah, some wives got beat up. There was one stabbing," says another staffer, Elaine, in a soft voice. "Nobody wants to think about those possibilities."

Another woman with a blonde ponytail and big black glasses explains to us, "Some of these wives are so young and so new to the Army. They're homesick and don't want to be in Germany. They spend all their time on Facebook. Some have never been away from their little home towns, and don't know how to make new friends."

Jane sighs. "The AFTB classes are so helpful, if only they would sign up. They need to learn this stuff about the Army, and where they can get help."

I admire the persistence of these social service workers, frustrated in their efforts to smooth the way for soldiers and families. Then Elaine reminds us, "You know that last group of soldiers? They went on leave for a month. When they get back next week they'll probably raise more hell."

A lot of effort goes into trying to protect these young warriors from themselves, but it seems that the Merks rarely succeed in interacting with them because the troops are too busy seeking further rushes of adrenaline. I've read that time spent in a combat zone can be emotionally destabilizing to these young people, and they often return changed — angry and bitter about their confusing experiences, shocked by what they've seen, numb and unwilling to discuss their feelings. And the Army expects them to shake this off and resume lives as happy, healthy spouses and parents. If only they could talk through these rough times, they might reach a state of greater emotional peace. I hope I can help here.

Soon another group of soldiers returns from a combat zone. They must face a checklist of dozens of tasks for completion within the first week back on base, from medical screenings to weapons check-in. On Reintegration Day Four, a day-long series of mandatory briefings takes place at the chapel, and the Base Chaplain invites me to come along. Topics include brain injury, financial matters, domestic violence, sexual assault, and typical family issues they may encounter. We deliver advice on avoiding risky behavior, a problem for young people returning from a violent situation. They have to re-learn how to drive in the civilian world, with less speed and aggression. Many have heard this information repeatedly, but they sit politely and endure it. At the end of the day, chaplains lead small group discussions to encourage talk about feelings related to deployment or the aftermath.

One of the battalion chaplains invites me to join a group. As I take a seat in a circle of folding chairs, I scan the insignia on the soldiers' shirtfronts and see I'm with a group of eight enlisted men . The man next to me, a staff sergeant, greets me and I guess that he's the leader of this small group.

"I'm a Merk," I say to him. "So, you all are just back?"

"That's right. Fourth day, and the last of the mandatory meetings! Then we'll put on civilian clothes and have a month of leave time."

"Do you have any special plans?"

"Not yet, but I'm sure my wife is cooking up something to do with the kids."

"Not your first deployment, I imagine?"

"Hell, no. It was my fourth. It's getting old. It's hard on the family."

"Will you re-enlist?"

"Oh, sure. In nine years I can retire. And in the meantime, I've got job security and we've got health insurance. Besides, I really don't know what I'd do as a civilian at this point." He pauses. "Being a soldier kind of takes over your life."

The man to my left is a private, slouched in his chair, looking at the floor. I turn to him and ask, "Was this your first deployment?"

"Yes."

He looks dejected, pre-occupied. I muse on the fact that deployments to Iraq and Afghanistan in the past year have typically been for fifteen months — a long time to live in extreme temperatures, tense with the possibility of being blown up at any moment.

"Are you married?" I ask.

He gives me a hard look. "I'm not sure any more. We got married just before I left and now she's..." His voice trails off. I just have time to hand him my card as the chaplain returns to start the meeting.

Since no one has yet called me on my well-publicized cell phone, I'm at a loss as to how to make myself useful on the base. But in the evenings and on the weekends I'm free to explore the town and experience modern German culture. This is the unexpected gift in my travels. I attend a concert of the Salzburg Mozart Quartet in the open air beside an ancient princely palace. The Bamberger Rudergesellschaft rowing club welcomes me to row with them one Saturday on the river that runs through town. I sign up for an Army-sponsored whitewater kayaking day trip on the Wiesen River and return joyfully exhausted. And I'm delighted by the town's annual Sandkerwa Volksfest, when for three days long tables are spread throughout the narrow streets of the old town, and people drink beer, eat potato pancakes, and listen to free popular concerts. I see no aggressive rowdiness, just a lot of happy drunken singing. Also, I am provided a rental car and per diem to cover meals and other expenses. Every morning I'm served an extensive tasty buffet in my hotel's sunny breakfast room. Who could complain?

One day, Karen tells me she's heard of a great German spa about twenty miles outside Bamberg and asks me if I want to go. She's nervous about not speaking any German, but I'm excited to explore the countryside. We arrive to find acres of landscaped grounds with many outdoor pools of healing mineral water at various temperatures. My German is barely good enough to read the signs listing entrance fees, but we needn't have worried — the staff speak English. We are pleased to learn that we can spend the whole day and evening, including entrance to Saunaland and use of a fluffy white terrycloth robe, for a surprisingly low fee. We change into our bathing suits in the spacious and immaculately clean blue-tiled locker room, and then explore the outdoor pools. The August sun is bright and there is a gentle breeze. Many of the guests here are older German couples taking the waters. In one large pool people are standing in chest-high water, following the postures of a tai chi instructor on the pool deck. Their graceful unison movements make me think of a ballet.

Inside an airy high-ceilinged building we find more attractive pools in various sizes. We are curious about Saunaland, so we pass through a door marked textile-frei (clothing-free) and enter a large open area. Here men and women can hang up their bathing suits and robes, shower, and try out the various sauna rooms which are held at different temperatures, some with soft music inside and some with colored lights. Being naked in this space feels completely natural and free. There is also a cold pool which connects with a private outdoor area, so one swims into the daylight where there is a poolside bistro. Karen and I fetch our robes, order a beer, and then have lunch. At the end of the afternoon we leave in a state of complete relaxation and bliss.

Weekdays on the base are a stark contrast. Walking by the blocky buildings housing families of enlisted personnel, I am overcome with the smell of Bounce fabric softener coming from the dryer vents and by the sound of screaming unruly children. I overhear ill-tempered wives gossiping about the people they share stairwells with. Some rarely leave the base, and few would ever go to a spa where nudity is permitted. I am assaulted by the smell of overheated grease coming from Popeye's. My deepest values — preserving natural beauty, enjoying cultural riches of art, architecture, music, eating healthy food, promoting cross-cultural understanding and world peace, intellectual honesty and speaking truth to power — find little validation on the base. I am repulsed by widespread mindless consumption of sugar and fat, gas-guzzling vehicles, X-rated pop culture, junky plastic goods, garish cheap clothing — all the horrors that are only minimally present in the privileged small college town where I live in the States.

I'm alarmed by the Christian fundamentalism being preached

at the chapel. I'm confounded by meeting people who believe not only that war is a viable option, but also that the U.S. is superior to other countries. I'm still troubled by the statement I heard at lunch, the belief that Muslims want to take over the U.S. and impose their religion. Where did that man get this idea, I wonder?

I ponder my reactions and am mortified that I am so judgmental. I reflect that my values are not likely to change, but try to remember that my tastes and education do not make me a superior person. I keep my thoughts to myself and try to keep my heart open. I can't imagine making the choice for military service myself, but the U.S. is fortunate that there are people willing to sign away their liberty out of a sense of duty, or for a certain compensation . Still, I know that their courage and willingness can be misused in reckless and futile military pursuits . The soldiers do not publicly question these pursuits, nor do they engage in political speech.

The on-base experience for me continues to be one of confusion and consternation, almost a sense of incarceration. But two events help me understand better what Army life is like at this time for those who have agreed to it. I'm invited to attend the family farewell of a contingent of soldiers on their way to Iraq. At 9 on a Thursday evening, two hundred soldiers line up in formation on the asphalt outside the motor pool, and each one is handed written orders. They've been in preparation mode for several weeks, but for security reasons, the precise time of departure is not announced until very close to the hour. Each one carries a small rucksack, a duffel bag, and a rifle on a shoulder strap. The bulk of their gear is already stowed in trailers. They're told they have until 1 a.m. to make last-minute preparations and say goodbyes.

Some have no families here and cluster in small groups. Some sit alone. Others have wives and children who have come to be with them. Some have been downrange before; for others it is their first time in a war zone. The atmosphere is peaceable and relaxed, reminding me of a small town homecoming dance, with young people joking and laughing in the shadows, some couples embracing. I hear no bravado in their voices. There is a gentleness, a sweetness that is especially poignant, knowing they are departing to a harsh environment where they risk being killed at any time. A group of spouses has set up a table with a variety of snacks, and soldiers come and go from the softly-lighted motor pool area. At 1 a.m. they get back into formation, a sergeant thanks the civilians present for their support, and there is a roll call. As each soldier's name is called, he or she shouts some sort of response and files off into the fenced motor pool yard. We see them lining up to choose MRE's (meals-ready-to-eat) to take with them on their journey. At 3 a.m. they will board buses with trailers in tow and head for Ramstein Air Base, from which they will be flying to Kuwait. There they will have a period of desert training and acclimatizing before their final destination in Iraq. I silently say a prayer for their protection.

A few days later, I attend my first military memorial service. A random rocket hit the tent of Sergeant First Class Jackson, in Iraq on his first combat assignment. The photo on an easel at the front of the chapel shows a dark-skinned Black man with a wide, smooth forehead and deep-set, kind-looking eyes. After the chaplain's remarks, there is another roll call:

"Sergeant Jones."

"Present, Sir."

"Sergeant Garcia."

"Present, Sir"

"Sergeant Jackson."

(no reply)
"Sergeant Jackson."
(no reply)
"Sergeant Jackson."
(no reply)

I hear a slow series of three rounds of gunfire outside the building. We then file forward to pay final respects to his picture and the emblems of his trade — the helmet, boots and rifle. I never knew the man, but cannot help but cry for his sacrifice, and for his wife and five children.

My six-week rotation comes to an end without my getting any formal requests for counseling. Packing my bags to return home, I ponder once again the question that has been with me the whole time: What is the Army? From what I've seen so far, it is an archaic behemoth, spread around the world, steeped in tradition and mired in bureaucracy. It is the employer of many fine people as well as some selfish bigots. It's such a large phenomenon that it seems impossible to get a view of its totality. What I can see, though, is that it is definitely not a lean, mean, fighting machine. And I remain baffled as to how my presence here could be truly beneficial.

CHAPTER 3

REINTEGRATION

2008

After six weeks away, I unlock the door to my house and almost fall into it. Someone I knew only slightly was housesitting, and I detect an unfamiliar odor. Perhaps she had a male visitor, or a pet? I open the windows and air the place out, eager to reclaim my home territory. Jet lag and time change have once again thrown off my circadian rhythms, and I sleep odd hours for the first week, stay in my pajamas all day, and talk over the phone with only a couple of friends. I feel as though I'm walking through a waking dream. I'm ungrounded, flapping in the breeze. My first assignment was more enjoyable than traumatic, yet the shock of total immersion in the military culture has left me reeling, my mind a chaotic tumble of thoughts and feelings. For six weeks I have observed what military people do and how they live in this time of endless war. My eyes have been opened to the stress put on a very small percentage of the country's population, about whom I knew so little before beginning this work. Now I've done enough reading to believe even more strongly that war is unnatural, inhumane, and hell, and that thousands of Americans are being exposed to it daily and are changed forever.

I continue to feel disoriented, as though something has changed and my identity has shifted. I dream of an orchestra performing an overture — to what I do not know. Something new is happening to me. My work is away from home, and my home has become a place to visit and relax. I remember soldiers saying their first visit to a supermarket after deployment blew them away — the refrigerated aisles, the endless array of breakfast cereals, so unlike the meager choices of food for the residents of impoverished Afghanistan and war-torn Iraq. Similarly, I now see my town from a new perspective. Everyone here seems so wealthy, self-involved, and oblivious to soldiers' deployments to far-flung wars.

Except to buy groceries, for two weeks I hardly leave the house. Despite seeing no clients in Bamberg, the daily and often confusing interaction with strangers for six weeks has drained me, and I desperately need time alone to recover my balance. I try to find my way back to balance through words. I'm reading Pico Iyer's *Global Soul*, intrigued by his sense of being a man without a nation, a citizen of the world. I'm also reading *Achilles in Vietnam* by Jonathan Shay, about trauma and betrayal, grief, and loss. I'm reading Emerson on "Self-Reliance." I'm journaling frantically, trying to make some sense out of where I've been and what I've been doing. My friend Barbara throws a welcome home party for me — and like the soldiers, I am embarrassed, feeling I didn't do much of importance while I was away. It is wonderful, however, to be affirmed in person by the people who have been receiving my emails and sending me so much love and encouragement in reply.

In Germany I made some calls to Malwell to see what assignments were coming up. As contractors, we may accept or refuse any assignments that are offered. They asked if I would go to Fort Drum in the fall. It was easy to say yes, since I'd heard Northern New York state is beautiful at any time. Fall must be astounding, but by the time I got home my assignment had been switched to two six-week rotations in Kentucky, not starting until late November. I agree to this, glad to have a three-month break at home.

At the end of October I sign up for a four-day Buddhist retreat in the woods at nearby Buckhorn Springs. I leave behind ordinary reality and enter a world of Tibetan Buddhist teachings. The setting at the springs is profoundly beautiful. The yellow leaves of tall oak trees rustle constantly and fall all around us; a stream rushes nearby. We live simply, in cabins, and eat the chef's finest vegetarian meals. My two American lamas from the refuge vow ceremony preside at the retreat, wearing maroon robes. They offer hours of lectures and discussion each day, and numerous periods of silent meditation.

We study the set of teachings called The Seven Points of Mind Training, brought to Tibet from India centuries ago. These are instructions on how to lead a good life, condensed to such a degree that each of the 59 "slogans" needs to be unpacked for its many layers of meaning. For instance, these include: "Always maintain a joyful mind," "Abandon all hope of fruition," and "Take adversity onto the path." The teachers explain the deeper meaning of these sayings, and also teach us a special meditation practice called *tonglen*, or "taking and sending." In this practice we imagine breathing the pain of others into our own boundless loving heart, where it is transformed into a peaceful vapor, then exhaled to bring greater peace into the world.

As the retreat progresses, I go further and further into a peaceful, altered state. This practice and these teachings are a gift to me as I seek some way to handle the adversity of traveling among strangers, acting as a witness to people fighting wars, and feeling uncertain I'll be able to help them. Becoming comfortable with uncertainty is on my path. I resolve to learn more about Buddhism — to study what's called the *dharma* — and try to rely on the teachings in my next assignment.

When the retreat is over, I continue to celebrate what seems like the most glorious fall of my life. In my walks around town, the colors make me gasp and stop, watching summer dying in a splendid bouquet of fire. I use my time off to drive to Los Angeles to visit my mother in her retirement home and arrive in time to celebrate Obama's election with a gaggle of aging Democrats. We sing "Happy Days Are Here Again!" and toast with champagne.

Once I return home, I have ten days to prepare for Kentucky. I repack my bags with warm winter clothes, close up the house, and I'm off to Fort Knox. Will there be gold there?

CHAPTER 4

CHRISTMAS IN THE TRENCHES

2008–2009

Someone is pounding on the door and shouting, "Housekeeping!" I know this is a ruse. No one would come to my hotel door this late at night. I don't answer it. *I'll call the front desk and report this.* But the light peeking in at the edge of the windows shows it's morning and I've been dreaming. Where am I? What time is it? The room is drab and dark. I stagger to the window and open the heavy drapes. A dozen large metal poles tower above me, a forest of them hundreds of feet high. At the top of each is a sign: "Texas Roadhouse," "La Quinta Inn," "Cracker Barrel," "Hampton Inn." My hotel is set in an enormous parking lot alongside a freeway interchange. Cars stream by on I-65, headed north to Louisville and south toward Bowling Green.

I make coffee in my room overlooking the bustling parking lot in central Kentucky. Last night I flew in to Louisville and drove the rental car to my hotel in Elizabethtown, but I don't see any town. It seems that this artificial village by the freeway has sprung up to serve visitors to Fort Knox, twenty miles north. This is my second assignment as a civilian Merk and my first inside the U.S.

It's Sunday, so I have the day to reconnoiter and do some provisioning before reporting to the base tomorrow. Cruising around in my bright red rental car, I discover Elizabethtown a mile or two west. A couple of large chain supermarkets, a few restaurants, a Chinese buffet. Old, modest houses near the center of town. A couple of new subdivisions. Banks made of red brick with large white Grecian columns out front — solid, Southern places to keep your money. Strip malls. None with a health food store. Or yoga studio. The town is without a pedestrian-friendly downtown shopping area.

And I am amazed to learn that there is nowhere to buy liquor because this is a dry county. I did not know there were still places like this in the United States. Well, to be precise, I'm told, it's a "moist" county, because certain restaurants are allowed to sell liquor by the drink along with their meals. But to buy a bottle of wine, or beer, or whisky for home consumption, it's a ten-mile drive into the next county to a liquor store. I decide to ask directions to such a store from the man behind the Papa Murphy's Pizza counter. I can see he does not approve of my errand, but he politely tells me how to get there and calls me "ma'am." It's a pleasant drive down a winding small country road with rambling ranch-style houses on either side. Only a few campaign signs remain in people's yards, and they urge a vote for the McCain/Palin Republican ticket. I'm not in Oregon anymore.

As promised, at the ten-mile marker is a low, drab building advertising "Liquor." I'm in the market for a couple of bottles of wine to take back to the hotel, and maybe a small bottle of Kentucky bourbon. Once inside, I'm hit by a wave of unease, but I don't know where it is coming from. The men behind the counter eye me briefly, then go back to their conversation. The other patrons seem lost in their own sad and hazy world. Then I get it. What I think I'm sensing is a combination of alcoholism and despair. As I pay for my purchase, I am self-conscious about my Yankee accent, and leave the store quickly. There is no joy here. No wine and cheese tasting. No olives or gourmet crackers.

It's time for dinner, so I head back to town to try out the Happy Family Chinese buffet. An astonishing variety of dishes sits in rows on steam tables that seem to go on endlessly. It's hard to choose, harder not to overeat. I roll out of there an hour later, satiated, a weak grin on my face.

Back in the motel room, I flip through the TV channels, landing on a local cable station replaying footage of a Veterans' Day parade and celebration held here last week. It's a big affair, not surprising in a community where fifty percent of people have a military connection. Children, flags, balloons, floats, open cars with honored guests, marching bands. Lots of old soldiers in their flat-folding garrison caps with VFW logos. Patriotic speeches. A young white man begins to sing, "I Am an American Christian," a song unfamiliar to me:

In God I will trust. And united I'll stand,
With my brothers and sisters, all over this land.
I love the Lord. I love the US of A.
It's the land of the free, of sweet liberty,
And I'm not ashamed to say:

> *(chorus) I'm an American Christian, born in the US of A.*
> *American Christian, born again by God's grace.*
> *And I thank God for my country, I can worship and pray.*
> *American Christian, lovin' my Jesus, in the US of A....*

By the time he gets to the second chorus, the crowd is aroused, cheering, Amen-ing. He's singing what they believe. By that time my heart is pounding in fear of these people, who have completely conflated the ideas of Christianity and patriotism. These clean-cut, smiley-faced people seem certain that God and Jesus are firmly on the side of the American military. Fighting for one's country is done in the name of Jesus, as an act of religious service. Christianity has been weaponized. When I turn off the television, I can't fall asleep. I quiet myself by reading my new president's biography, *Dreams from my Father,* and turn out the light.

In the morning, I get into my rental car and head north to Fort Knox on US31-W, part of the historic Dixie Highway. This is a two-lane road, a twenty-mile commercial strip of small businesses catering to the needs of military families. A lot of tanning salons and used furniture stores. I wonder if I should try the Heavenly Ham at Hungry Howie's. A Mexican restaurant is offering $1.99 lunchtime margaritas. A couple of no-tell motels.

I get off the highway on Bullion Boulevard and stop at the visitors' center to get an I.D. card permitting me to enter this large military base. A long, low stone building sits a few hundred yards to the left, surrounded by fences and razor wire. The U.S. Bullion Depository, operated by the Treasury Department, permits no visitors. It looks deserted. A lot of gold is supposedly stored underground there. I later learn that it is guarded by the U.S. Mint Police. I picture tiny guards in mint green uniforms. My assignment does not include this building since it is not under military jurisdiction. Each time I pass it in the coming weeks, I will become more doubtful that anything is inside.

Once I've entered the base, I seek out the Army Community Services office, which here is a low wooden building down by the railroad tracks. As I push open the creaking door of what must have been a "temporary" structure installed during World War II, I find a large room filled with many desks. A din of conversation rises from the dozen or more people working here.

"I'm the new Merk," I say to the first person who makes eye contact.

"Sure, sure. You want to see Donna, over there in the red dress." She's indicating a tall, slender blonde woman in high heels, wearing a stylish red wool dress with a wide black patent leather belt.

Donna is expecting me. She smiles and extends her hand. "I'm Donna — the ACS Director. You must be Maureen." She makes a sweeping gesture. "Welcome to our humble quarters. I'll be your POC."

"Pleased to meet you," I say, shaking her hand.

"Don't take off your coat. We're due for a meeting with Hank, the MWR Director. He's making a presentation about next year's budget, and *everyone* is going to be there. Come on, I'll drive," she says, putting on her full-length woolen coat. In this latest acronym, Hank's the Morale, Welfare, and Recreation chief.

On the way to the meeting, she looks over at me. "You're going to really like Hank. He's a great guy." Looking back at the road, she smiles mysteriously. "He's going to be getting ACS some *much* classier office space in the new MWR building. We've been in that bungalow for years. Years! We can barely fit everyone in anymore." She makes a quick turn into a large parking lot. "And it's so drafty in the winter."

We enter a large multi-purpose room with heavy-duty vinyl flooring, where dozens of folding chairs have been set out. A tall, heavy-set white man in a long-sleeved white shirt and tight-fitting trousers has his hand on the side of a podium, talking with several others. Donna finds us seats as close as possible to the front, then approaches him. I can't hear what they're saying, but from the angle of her head and the animated swaying of her body, I would guess she's flirting. By the look on his face, he doesn't mind a bit.

Soon we are listening to his enthusiastic speech promoting ideas for a major expansion of sports facilities for military families at Fort Knox. He shows us slides with diagrams and cost figures. The numbers seem shockingly high, many millions of dollars. Hasn't anyone heard about the financial market meltdown, the crashing recession? His proposals seem to fly in the face of current economic realities and assume that the flow of money to support any and all military projects is not only deserved but endless and guaranteed. Though he alludes to a vague apprehension that "the new administration" may not fully support all things military, his staff continue to dream up new ways of spending taxpayer dollars. I am within the belly of the Republican military beast. Belt-tightening will not be required. I feel queasy. I am deep in the flag-waving South — an alternative universe contrasted with my liberal West Coast culture.

Donna drops me off back at the ACS office and goes on to other errands, promising to meet me at the end of the day for further orientation. It's freezing outside, but I go for a walk. I've got to get some fresh air. My thoughts are churning. I'm still quaking from watching last night's American Christians. I see them as being in a trance, convinced of some strange beliefs about who's in charge of this life. Apparently, from there it's a mere step to believing that your way is the only way and getting really pushy about your religion and deciding that there's a battle between God and the Devil, and if you're not on God's side you must be doing the work of the Devil and need to be excluded, or avoided, or punished. Especially Muslims. Some people in these parts believe all Muslims hate us and want to bring down Western civilization. They won't allow it. They will mount a crusade against Islam and wipe it from the face of the earth! My God, the Crusades all over again. Deep breath, Maureen.

I have nothing to do for the rest of the day, so I drive about, exploring the base. Fort Knox is huge in comparison with the little German garrison, and with the headquarters of several Army units here, there is a ponderous sense of permanence, entrenchment, military might. Large buildings, mostly brick, with a few sorry wooden structures left over from WWII, are scattered over several square miles. North of the base there are 177 more square miles of woods and fields used for training in vehicular warfare (tanks, hummers, etc.) and artillery. One hears occasional far-off booming and banging. Recruits in basic training march about, counting cadence. In Bamberg, career soldiers had told me, "This is not the real Army," expressing their views about the sloppy discipline and lack of mission focus there. This fire-and-brimstone culture and reverence for authority at Fort Knox more closely express the essence of Army.

Within a few days, my empty calendar shows my latest assignment will make few demands. Almost no one calls to request a counseling session. Each week I must give one five-minute briefing to soldiers newly arrived at the base. They sit passively in a small room while we civilians parade in with information about various base services. I wait my turn just outside the door, fascinated by a cardboard cut-out of a fresh-faced, happy-looking white soldier in full combat uniform. About three-quarters life-size, he stands in the hallway with his rifle. At the other end of the corridor stands his female counterpart. I'm not sure why they're here, but they look friendly and I ask someone to take my picture with each of them.

I hear frequent references to soldiers as "warfighters," emphasizing the lethality of their job. The Army has been on a war footing for years by now, and no one is more aware of this than military personnel and their families. They live in a world different from mine and that of my friends. In my Oregon town, military families are invisible. From world and national news we all learn that people from around the country are risking their lives in Iraq or Afghanistan. But they are usually strangers to us. We rarely ponder what their lives are like.

I'm grateful to discover I have access to the base library, which is full of timely books, videos, and audio recordings. I research the Iraq and Afghanistan wars through DVDs and accounts written by journalists and soldiers in the field. I sense less secretiveness from the Army itself than from the military-industrial-financial-corporate-governmental complex. These interest groups outside the Army actually pull the soldiers into conflicts and influence decisions about how long they remain there, under what rules of engagement. These huge economic and political forces are largely hidden from us.

ONE PARTICULAR TASK FOR MERKS AT FORT KNOX is to work with soldiers who did not make it through basic training — either because they had a bad reaction to Army discipline; displayed incorrigibly bad attitudes; committed crimes like selling drugs; were discovered to have pre-existing medical conditions that were unknown or undisclosed at induction; or were injured during training (like falling while on an obstacle course). This group is all male, but otherwise diverse and constantly changing as they are processed and finally discharged.

It is odd and uncomfortable at first for me to be in the midst of this unit. The still-privates-not-yet-civilians are held without liberty, restricted to a barracks building, required to jump to attention, and request permission to speak to superiors. They get barked at by drill sergeants. It all seems a little silly, since they are no longer in training to become soldiers, but as a guest in this setting, I refrain from commenting on this. These soldiers languish in limbo with nothing to do, occasionally permitted to watch television as they wait for the slow wheels of military bureaucracy to grind out their fate.

On one visit, I notice a young Black soldier sitting with his head on the table. When he looks up, I slide in beside him.

"Who you?" he says, startled.

"I'm a counselor. I'm here to talk to anyone, if they want to talk."

"A counselor. I know about that, yeah, I know about that. What you want?"

"Nothing really. How are you doing? How'd you end up here?"

He shakes his head, once, twice, and again, as though trying to shake something out of his head. "I can't be here anymore. I miss my home. I'm scared. I want to go back to the group home, back to L.A."

"You were in a group home?"

"Yeah, for people like me that's schizophrenic. I didn't like it there much, but this ... this is terrible. The recruiter said, he told me, 'Don't tell them about your diagnosis, then everything will be fine.'"

"I guess it didn't turn out so fine."

"Naw, they always yelling at me. I can't take it. I gotta rest now." He turns away and puts his head back on the table. The recruiter took this man out of a home for the mentally ill? They were that desperate to meet their quotas? I'm told there has been a rash of suicide amongst the recruiters due to the pressure of meeting quotas. After I learn that, I want to put my head on the table, too.

One evening, I have dinner with another Merk who's been on the base for six weeks and is about to leave. He is a well-dressed, balding, business-minded consulting psychologist. He's done this work for three years and I pick his brain about how to survive as an independent contractor, dealing with the big corporation. He doesn't have nearly the difficulty I do, since he has no fundamental objections to corporate America or to military culture. In response to my complaints about how we are kept in the dark and treated by Malwell in a high-handed way , he says simply, "Corporations don't care about people. They have to make money for their shareholders." He advises me that if I get another European assignment, I should know that the only acceptable answer when we are asked during the debriefing to summarize our experience is this: "Our program was well received, and it was a life-changing experience for me personally." Any sort of thoughtful criticism or suggestions would be highly unwelcome. He doesn't even sound cynical as he says this, just matter-of-fact.

The late November weather has been cold, dark, and windy. Longing for a way to be outdoors on the weekends rather than cooped up in my hotel room, I cross the parking lot into an adjacent field and trudge in the daytime gloom through frozen clods of earth, seeking some natural beauty. I find only rusty train tracks and more muddy fields. The frozen outer world adds to my inner loneliness, my yearning for warmth.

In spite of myself, I start to dwell on my solitary status, the absence of a life partner. Normally I'd be able to shake off such self-pity and recognize it as a sign of depression. Instead my thoughts continue to drift to a sense of unfairness that I have been ten years without a relationship, and I feel increasingly morose. I forget to meditate, which would help me get some perspective on this negative thinking. My inflatable *zafu* cushion gathers dust in a corner.

An Army social worker invites me to spend Thanksgiving with her and her husband, a retired military officer now running a horse farm. I'm afraid to go, afraid I'll become hysterical amongst these conservative believers, afraid I'll be exposed as the commie hippie looney lesbian from the West Coast, the liberal unbeliever they've heard of but never met. I beg off and spend Thanksgiving at the hotel, warming up a pre-cooked turkey wing in the microwave. I am alone and friendless because these people scare me so much. And I'm disappointed in myself that I didn't choose to take the risk of being in an intimate setting with people so different from me. I spend the weekend reading, watching DVDs, and ranting privately about the military, complaining that it is bloated, gargantuan, impossibly huge. Inefficient, bureaucratic, self-serving, full of parasitical, entitled behaviors. I gnash my teeth and muse that to kill even one terrorist, the military must spend many millions of dollars.

For the next month I overeat, especially Chinese food and holiday candy. One cold evening I go to the Christmas tree lighting ceremony on base. Santa arrives in a horse-drawn carriage and admonishes us to be good. Free Christmas trees are distributed to all personnel courtesy of FedEx. Brownie scouts and high school students sing carols off-key. A small wind ensemble of the Army

Band plays gloveless in the 32-degree weather, led by a pinch-faced martinet conductor. The Base Commander speaks briefly, commending the soldiers for doing "the Lord's work." Really, he said that.

I'm bored. I've done what I could to drum up business, but none has come my way. I've abandoned hope of doing any good here, or making any sense of what the Army is all about. I am crashing into depression, yet I keep looking outside myself for a remedy. The venerable Abbey of Gesthemani is only a short drive from Elizabethtown. I was moved by Thomas Merton's autobiography describing his conversion to Catholicism and becoming a priest, so I am curious to see the place where he spent years of his life. I have found inspiration in the practices and holy places of many religions.

When I get to the Abbey, the ivy-covered stone stairways and passages of my imagination are nowhere to be seen. The monastery sits atop a small hill covered with grass, now brown and dead. A low retaining wall encloses the monastery. Most of the grounds are closed to the public. The monks pray formally several times a day, and welcome visitors to sit in on these services in a chapel just outside the cloistered area. Due to Merton's fame, many visitors come each year and a small shop is open to sell books as well as products made by the monks. In the shop I spot a monk, a tall man in a white cassock, with curly dark hair and a short beard. He looks kind and I approach him.

"Would I be able to talk to you?" I ask.

"Yes, certainly. Come and have a seat." We sit together on an upholstered bench at the back of the store.

"I'm working at Fort Knox, at the Army base."

"Oh, yes."

"I'm just there for a few weeks. I'm a counselor. But I feel so out of place. I've always been opposed to war, but I took this job and ... I don't know. I feel conflicted inside." I ramble on, trying to find words for my state of mind, not sure what I'm looking for.

He listens attentively, patiently. After a pause he says, "God speaks to each of us individually and wants us to be ourselves." He smiles gently, then excuses himself as he has some other business. I sit there a few minutes in the well-lighted shop, listening to a soft murmur of voices, turning over the monk's words in my mind. I help myself to a cup of complimentary Monastery Coffee, then buy a pound, along with a book on loneliness called *The Restless Heart*. I decide to sit in on the vespers service about to start in the chapel, but this does not provide the solace I'm seeking. I drive slowly back to the hotel. The next morning, sitting on my meditation cushion, I find myself in tears. I feel alone and wish for some kind of comfort. All I know how to do is to pray for guidance, illumination, protection, and freedom from fear. This helps me to remember that this state of mind is not permanent and at some point will pass.

I cannot bear the idea of spending Christmas in this alienated and lonely state of mind. I am not Catholic, and every other Christian church in Elizabethtown is aligned with the conservative, fundamentalist position I find infuriating: "The Bible is the inerrant word of God." No, I would not feel comfortable among evolution-denying, anti-homosexual believers who endorse the apocalyptic visions of the Book of Revelations and the imminent, literal second coming of Christ.

I search the internet for Unitarian Universalists, the liberal denomination known for its inclusive and eclectic celebration of all spiritual paths. Two UU congregations are listed in Louisville, the city of 700,000 that is fifty miles to the north. In early December, I decide to visit the smaller of these two churches, and take the hour-long drive on a Sunday morning. I find a tiny white clapboard church with its small steeple on a corner in an old residential neighborhood.

"Hello, good morning, welcome to Clifton Universalist," says a white-haired man with military bearing standing at the entrance. He offers a warm handshake, saying, "We're always glad to see a new face." He shows me into the large linoleum-floored room that serves as both sanctuary and social hall. About a dozen white people of all ages are gathered, dressed casually. They are helping themselves to coffee from an ancient urn that sits on the pass-through counter connecting to a tiny kitchen. I'm about to take a cup myself when I see the big jar of Cremora and change my mind. I'm partial to half and half.

A young woman with large brown eyes is wearing a floor-length cotton skirt and a bulky red sweater. On her head is a Peruvian knitted hat with tassels dangling from the ear covers. When we make eye contact, she approaches me and smiles. "I'm River," she says, and I introduce myself as a visitor temporarily working at Fort Knox.

"You mean like the military?" she says, her eyes growing even wider.

"Yes, but I'm not in the service. I'm a psychologist, just there for a few weeks."

"That's cool. My grandfather was in the Vietnam War. He got PTSD."

Grandfather? Oh honey, you're making me feel so old.

The service is about to start and we all find seats in the pews at the carpeted end of the room. A teenage boy lights the ritual chalice candle. The hymns are blessedly free of references to Lord,

Him, the blood of the Lamb, or salvation from sin. Instead we sing, "God of the sparrow, God of the whale, God of the swirling stars." The young male minister, fresh out of seminary, steps up to the lectern. He uses a Rumi poem as his text. He speaks of the birth of Jesus as being a metaphor for the returning of hope in dark times. I appreciate his suggestion that the Christmas season is a time to slow down, to look inward to find our essential loving nature, and to allow that love to manifest in the world. I find comfort in his message and his thoughtful and gentle delivery, and also from being with others who have gathered for community and inspiration.

I stay and have a cup of tea, listening to women talk about their work at a local food pantry.

"We had to stay open an extra hour just to get everyone in the door. The shelves are getting empty."

"It's the recession. People who've never been out of work before can't pay their bills, so they're grateful for a box of food."

"I love helping out there, though. I feel I'm doing something that matters, that gives people what they really need."

There is a balm in Louisville, and I have found it here at this church. The people's welcome, openness, and genuine caring help heal my ragged soul. I want to return, and I do. On my third visit, I work up the courage to speak of my loneliness and isolation to people gathered for coffee after the service.

"Well, you shouldn't be alone at Christmas," says Marty, a small, vivacious woman with brilliantly white curly hair. She grabs the arm of a tall man in a gray tweed jacket, who is standing nearby. "Kent, let's have Maureen come to our house for Christmas."

"Oh, sure. That would be real nice," he says. "Our kids live in California and Minnesota and nobody's coming this year. It's just us."

Marty is enthusiastic. "You can come and spend the night. We live just across the river from here, in Indiana. I'll draw you a map." I can hardly speak I'm so grateful.

Later that week on December 24, I drive across the Ohio river to New Albany, Indiana. I find Marty and Kent's house in a neighborhood with old pickup trucks on muddy driveways and kids' plastic toys scattered on the lawns. "Our kids thought we were making a mistake to live here," Marty tells me as she shows me around the house. "But it's actually very safe, and the neighbors are friendly. It's unpretentious."

"See the long narrow floorplan?" Kent adds. "It's what they call a shotgun house. I guess because you could shoot a gun right down the hall from one end to the other."

The small house is beautiful, unlike any I've ever seen. Marty is an artist, and has decorated inside and out with quirky found objects, old bottle glass, pieces of folk art, ceramic suns, and vigorous houseplants. I take many photographs of this unique dwelling place.

We sit down to eat the salmon dinner that Marty has cooked, and I learn that they are both retired social workers. They ask about my work. We talk politics, and share our delight in anticipating what Obama's presidency might accomplish. Then they show me to their small bedroom and say, "This is where you'll sleep. We've got another bed in the attic and we'll sleep there." These folks look to be in their late seventies or older. I protest that at their age they have no business climbing the steep ladder and I will gladly sleep upstairs. They are insistent, and will not let me interfere with their choice as hosts. I give in and accept the lesson in generosity and hospitality.

On Christmas morning, we have Kent's excellent strong coffee, and Marty makes us pancakes. "Gluten-free!" she crows, having heard about my dietary needs. Afterward, we get comfortable in the living room and watch *Garbage Warriors,* a documentary about a New Mexico architect who builds self-sustaining houses with creatively recycled materials. We resonate with the values of innovation, artistic expression, environmental preservation, and sheer quirkiness. I have felt so starved for companionship that affirms my deepest values. I breathe a huge sigh of relief. *These are my people.*

It's a sunny afternoon, so they invite me to go with them to the nearby woods for a leisurely walk. I take more photos to remember these people and this day. After we get back to their house, I catch Kent vacuuming out my rental car. "We all had muddy feet," he explains, "especially the dog." When I cook them my favorite chicken curry recipe for dinner, they love it. They want me to stay another night but I don't want them to be displaced from their bed any longer, so I demur, telling them I have work I need to do. These kind people help me get through this time, showing that there can be hope and love even in the darkest winter in the conservative Heartland.

WRITING GROUP EMAILS TO MY FRIENDS and receiving their warm, encouraging replies is the other thing that has kept me going. I usually try to sound brave, but suspect they can read between the lines and know when I'm having a hard time. In my last post from Fort Knox I write:

Dear Friends—

It's very quiet and cold here in Kentucky, and Fort Knox is emptied out for the holidays; even the soldiers in basic training have been given leave. I'm left to muse on the cultural phenomenon of Christmas in all its tarnished tinsel, wondering about that magic that's been so hyped and Disneyfied that it's hard to discern if there ever really was a beautiful and silent night. Our fast-moving society has certainly lost the innocence of a slower time, and my own inclination is to view it all as humbug.

But then I'll hear John McCutcheon's song "Christmas in the Trenches" and feel my heart caught in the timeless moment of love that appears at the very instant it seems all hope is lost. There really was a one-night sacred truce on the battlefield in 1914 when German and British soldiers sang "Silent Night" together. Listen to this heart-wrenching song when the moment seems right.

Every good wish to each of you to know the deep peace of midwinter, and to flow through this time gently, easily, trusting in the return of the light. May your heart be filled with wonder, with gratitude, with love. From my heart to yours — Maureen

CHAPTER 5

PRACTICE AT FORT CAMPBELL

2009

I leave Kentucky after New Year's and arrive home agitated and tense, worried that six days will not be enough time for rest and renewal before I must return to the military. My neck and shoulders ache terribly. After dumping my luggage at the house, I go to the Wellsprings Spa to swim in the pool and relax in the hot tub. I pick up essential groceries, and then my next-door neighbor invites me for a glass of wine. Soon I'm asleep at home but wake up at 5 a.m. to a dazzling full moon of historic closeness. I sit outside, bathing in the moonlight, feeling blessed by the rays, and blessed to have such a full life, even if it sometimes stretches me to the limit.

In sunny and unseasonably warm weather, I walk with a friend around Emigrant Lake, where I photograph the gleaming vermillion wild rose hips contrasting with the green and blue lines of lake, hills and sky. I write in my journal. I catch up with other friends during dates for dinner, lunch, and tea. I go to a Buddhist Calm Abiding meditation but my mind races wildly. I do not feel calm. In a crystal healing session with my massage therapist, I visit with my inner child who reminds me that I am an artist and it's okay to be different. In my women's support group meeting I feel disconnected, as though I'd died and now visit as a ghost. They support me anyway. I sing at a nursing home with seven friends from the Threshold Choir. I tell them I must be bilocating, seeing them as through a veil, not feeling fully present. Someone in Nashville winks at me on Match.com.

With two days remaining, I panic and dissolve, weeping as everything crashes in on me, and I am lost in clouds of dismay. I dream of being beaten up and trying to protect myself. I have not had enough time to fully recover. Nevertheless I pack up and fly to Nashville.

My assignment is Fort Campbell, which sits directly on the border of Kentucky and Tennessee. It is the second largest military installation in the country, with 30,000 soldiers, 55,000 family members, and many thousands of civilian employees. When I check in at the Candlewood Inn, there's a message that someone named Charlie in Room 202 wants me to call. I do and find he's the lead Merk.

"I thought you might want to know," he says, "that there's an opportunity Monday morning to meet a plane that's bringing soldiers home from Afghanistan. Some of the 101st Screaming Eagles. The plane's due in at 6:30, but generally families start gathering there about two hours early. Like around 4:30. Do you want to be one of the Merks to meet the plane?"

I completely hate the idea of getting up that early. I say, "Sure. Where do I go?"

"Come down to the lobby and I'll give you a map to the airfield."

The Candlewood caters to business clientele who may be in

the area for a few weeks or months. I'm impressed that I get not only a coffee maker, microwave and wi-fi, but also a range top, a sink, and a full-size refrigerator, plus a built-in table for eating or doing my paperwork. After one solid night's sleep, I have the day to myself on Sunday.

I run into another Merk, Marion, as she's checking in. I help her get her bags up to her room, which is on the floor above mine.

"I'm coming from Anchorage," she tells me, "but that's not actually my home. I've been up there six months working at Fort Richardson."

From the acrid, stuffy smell that greets us as the elevator opens at Level 3, I know this is the smoking floor. "You mean you've been there right through midwinter? Must've been cold!"

"It didn't start getting really cold until November."

"So you flew directly here? You didn't go home first to ...?"

"My home's in Wisconsin. But I had no time to go there if I wanted to be part of this Merk surge, and I do."

"A surge of Merks?"

"Didn't you know? That's why we're here. Malwell has sent in a dozen Merks on a special assignment to interview troops returning from deployment. I think at least three brigades have gotten back here in the last month, maybe five or ten thousand soldiers." She drops her bags in the room, sits on the arm of the overstuffed couch, lights a cigarette, and takes a deep drag. "I was at Fort Riley last year when we had the first surge, and it was amazing. The commander ordered every returning soldier to meet once with a Merk, and we managed to see thousands of them."

"What was that like?"

"Best assignment I've ever had. We just asked them to tell us how the deployment went, and then they told us. Mostly they were just glad to talk. Sometimes we gave them referrals; mostly we just listened. We were always busy, so it was a good gig. I think we were really helpful."

"No wonder I've seen so many Merks in this hotel. I would love to be busy. I had nothing to do at Fort Knox, where I just spent six weeks."

I get up at 3:30 a.m. on Monday after just a few hours' sleep and drive in the dark to the airfield. I find a large brightly-lit gymnasium with a polished wood floor, and people are milling around, some in uniform and some not. The walls are hung with red, white and blue "Welcome Home" banners, and children are waving homemade signs like "My Daddy Is My Hero." The room buzzes with excitement. I meet a Hispanic man who has flown in from Arizona in order to see his son the moment he arrives in the country. He wears a white sweatshirt with "ARMY" in big green letters. I take a seat on the bleachers and ask a well-dressed couple whom they're meeting. "Our son," says the man. "I came from Pennsylvania and she flew from California."

"We're not married anymore," she explains, "but we both love our son and want to see him home safe."

A talented singer-songwriter entertains us as we wait. Some Army Band members play jazzy dance music. The plane touches down promptly at 6:30 a.m., and once the soldiers enter the room, a huge cheer goes up. They have to stand in formation briefly while their commanders address the assembly and the chaplain says a prayer, then they're free for hugs, hurrahs, balloons, and tears. The joy and relief of seeing loved ones home from war is palpable, and tears form in my eyes, too. As a witness to this outpouring of love, I share everyone's relief that these soldiers have made it home from the war.

ON TUESDAY, WE HAVE OUR FIRST GENERAL MERK MEETING in the attractive, newly-constructed two-story brick building that houses all the ACS services for this enormous base. The mint-green-carpeted meeting room gradually fills with Merks, waving greetings to those they've met before, and seating themselves on the soft couches and upholstered chairs that surround a long low coffee table. Seven white men in casual slacks are wearing no-iron shirts open at the collar; two of them wear sports jackets. The youngest of the men wears a close-fitting black leather jacket and has some subtle gay mannerisms as well as a shaved head. Seven women also take their seats, dressed in flowing skirts or pressed slacks, with sweaters, scarves and tasteful jewelry. One is a striking, slender light-skinned African-American woman; the rest are white. Everyone appears to be at least over fifty, apart from the man in the black jacket. We are all wearing our oversize gold-colored plastic name tags inscribed with our name and "Military Resiliency Coach." I initially think my choice of a new cowl-necked dark teal sweater is a good one, but soon I am sweltering in its acrylic warmth designed for outdoor wear.

Our leader, Charlie, is a short, sturdy dark-haired Merk with a bristly mustache who has prior experience at this base, and he will coordinate our efforts. "Welcome, welcome everybody! Great to have you all here. Have you all settled in at the Candlewood? I'm staying there too, so if you need to find me, just ask at the desk."

He has us introduce ourselves, and we discover we are from all around the country: Louisiana, New York, Ohio, Wisconsin, Colorado, Tennessee, California, Oregon, and Texas. Some have Ph.D.s, others are masters-level social workers and counselors. One man is a retired Army colonel, formerly a Family Life Chaplain. Another is ordained in an evangelical denomination.

Except for Marion, none of us has worked a surge before, and people seem excited to be here.

Charlie's self-introduction is rambling, and covers how he joined the Coast Guard as a young man during the Vietnam era, thinking this would mean spending time in U.S. coastal waters. "Wow. It wasn't what I expected at all. I ended up in Honduras. Very tense. Drug lords and revolutionaries." His eagerness to bring us together as a group is charming, and his energy makes me think of a happy puppy.

"So the surge, Charlie, how is that going to work?" asks the retired colonel.

"Ah, well. It's not going to be like the one they had at Fort Riley, and that's really too bad. The 101st Airborne Division has its headquarters here, and three brigades just came back from Afghanistan. The DoD gave the go-ahead to Malwell to bring in all of you — a great opportunity to get these soldiers seen and screened after their deployments. And we can still see them. But the Division Commander decided just this week he didn't want to make the post-deployment interviews mandatory the way they were at Fort Riley. So it's up to the individual soldiers to decide whether they want to come in."

It takes a moment for the significance of this to sink in. I say, "I wonder how many of them will actually take the initiative — 10%? 5%? Why wouldn't the commander want to take advantage of our presence and order all of them to come in?"

Charlie shrugs. "He's old school, maybe. I'm guessing he thinks no soldier worthy of the name would want to talk about his feelings."

People are shaking their heads. I follow up. "So the Army says it's concerned about soldier stress, family stress, suicides, and brings in a bunch of extra counselors, then doesn't use them?"

"Wow," says another Merk. "And I just heard General Ham on television, a four-star general at the Pentagon, talking about how he got treatment for PTSD. He said, 'Don't keep things locked up inside. Use the services. Get help. You'll be a better soldier.'"

"It's all true," says Charlie. "But old attitudes die hard."

"Are we going to be sent home?"

"No, no. We're going to be creative about getting the job done another way. We've got the use of three offices here at ACS, and we'll rotate you into them to see soldiers on a drop-in basis." He flashes a new whiteboard intended for this purpose. "You can use the rest of your time going out and making casual contacts, seeking out people who could use our services. Lots of places you could go — the gyms, the DFACs, Starbucks. We'll set up some tables outside the Post Exchange. But you definitely can't hang out in this room or really anywhere in the ACS building except for in our office space. The POC doesn't want it to look like you're not busy." Maybe the POC thinks it would be bad for his own team's morale to see us strangers lolling about the place while they're busy doing their jobs.

Before I've had time to process this information or discuss it quietly with a colleague, the meeting is breaking up. Charlie shows us our offices, and makes a little chart where we can sign up to staff a few hours every week. We heed his warning to leave the building, and go out into the frigid day. The Merks scatter to their cars. I don't know where they're going, but I check my map for the location of the library. Seems like a place to start. A short drive up Screaming Eagle Boulevard takes me to the small R.F. Sink Memorial Library, the only one on base. It's quiet, with a handful of people using the public computers. The cramped little library's collection is meagre, specializing in popular fiction and blockbuster DVDs. Although Merks are allowed into this library, as contractors we have no check-out privileges. In the absence of any public areas to hang out, I can see this not a good place to encounter people in my role as Merk.

Over the next few days, I do a search for all possible locations where I could spend time angling to nab a soldier or spouse who'd like to talk about problems. The Malwell construct of "walking social work" seems especially ludicrous in this cold weather. Could it really be my job to hunt people down and try to make them talk? I find a few places where I can come in out of the cold to sit and look friendly, but what's the likelihood that someone on their way to work out at the gym would want to stop and talk to me? It's improbable, and I settle for just sitting there in the gym lobby, eating my breakfast from a plastic container: cold omelet, blueberries and yogurt. I strike up a conversation with the pony-tailed young white woman checking people in at the door, telling her who I am and why I'm here. She thinks that's really nice, but that's about the extent of it, and she's pretty busy.

I try similar stake-outs at the DFACs (Dining Facilities, known in former years as mess halls) and the food court.Contractors are not allowed inside the PX but at any point I'm free to join the bundled-up Merks standing outside by tables of literature, trying to get the attention of passers-by. Perhaps we need a bell to ring like the Salvation Army at Christmas. Our purpose there must seem obscure to the busy people. By the end of the week the absurdity of the situation begins to hit me, and I doubt that such strategies will ever result in any meaningful contacts. Somehow, I have to figure out where I can go to pass the time on base on weekdays for the next six weeks.

Charlie provides us with small "Need to Talk?" signs. I gladly set up one of the plexiglass holders on a table at Starbucks and sit there with a book, hoping I look approachable. That this idea of "need" might be off-putting to self-respecting warriors does not occur to me, and of course, no one comes to my table. So I drink coffee and read soldiers' memoirs and heartfelt journalism like Martha Raddatz's *The Long Road Home* about a unit of soldiers she covered through a lethal ambush in Baghdad in 2004. I learn something of what it is like to be a soldier in wartime and feel I'm preparing to better understand those who might seek me out. I absorb the turmoil and complexities of the military family experience in Tania Biank's *Army Wives*. When I feel up to it, I choose books about combat and PTSD. My studies lead to greater empathy for those I'm here to serve. I try to imagine that my presence in the coffee shop is somehow comforting.

When it's my turn to sit in the Merk office, I typically end up reading or chatting with other Merks. Then one day, it happens. A young soldier walks in, one with a sweet round face and dark hair that I think might be curly if he didn't have to keep it so short. Once I close the door he asks, "Can we talk about anything?"

"Sure. Anything that's on your mind."

He settles into a swivel chair and leans back. "I guess the main thing is my girlfriend. I can't stop thinking about her and worrying. She's deployed to Afghanistan."

"You must miss her. What do you mainly worry about?"

"She says she's fine, but I'm not sure. When you're over there you have to put your feelings aside, and not talk about them. I know, because I've been there myself, twice. She worried about me when I was deployed. It's a dangerous place."

He's a staff sergeant and tells me he's not yet thirty. He's opting to end his Army service next month when his second enlistment contract ends. "If I re-enlist, I'd have to go back to the war, and I've had enough. Her contract is up next year, and she's said she wants out, too. I'm ready to be a civilian again."

"How has it been for you, being in the Army?"

"Great. I've learned a lot about myself, gotten stronger. I'm really impressed with those First Sergeants, and the Command Sergeant Majors. Whew! They have so much focus, so much dedication. Here, look at this." He sits forward and shows me a small silver pin on the breast of his uniform. "My Air Assault wings. I took a ten-day course, and we learned about helicopter combat and how to insert and extract soldiers from the ground."

"That sounds intense. Was it hard?"

"Very hard. I had to work out and get in really good shape just to get ready for the class. But it really builds your self-respect and your confidence, too. You know, all us Airborne soldiers have to learn to jump from planes."

"That is such a big deal. I admire your courage. But getting back to your girlfriend, are you able to stay in touch with her while she's deployed?"

"We talk pretty much every day or two. Her job is inside the Forward Operating Base, so she always has access to phone or Skype. Honestly—" He pauses, clears his throat, looks down at the floor and says softly, "What I really worry about the most is that she could be, you know, talking to another guy."

"Oh yeah, I see," I say, matching his tone. "You've been deployed. You've probably seen that sort of thing happen."

"All the time. And even if it's not happening, people start rumors and put them on Facebook, like, he's sleeping with a girl in his unit, or, she's seeing someone back on base while her hubby is away. Then everybody freaks out."

"I get it. So you wonder if you can trust your girlfriend."

"I know I should trust her. She's such a great girl, really honest. We gave each other promise rings. Like, not engaged yet, but promising to be true to each other."

"Have you told her you worry about this?"

"I'll make a joke about it, but not seriously. I don't want her to know how obsessed I get. Then she'll ask me, well, what about you?"

"And?"

"I tell her, no of course not! I can't wait for her to be home again."

"Sure, but you're human too. Do you ever worry you won't keep your promise?"

"Nah, I'm good," he says, blushing. "I do have fun hanging out with those gals at the psychic bookshop in Nashville, but that's not where my heart is. I can definitely wait for her, I want to." He smiles. "You know, it's a relief to talk about this. The Army taught me to set aside fear and be confident. I need to trust us both more."

"I think you nailed it. Trust is a wonderful thing, and sometimes you have to work on it. But if you're clear where your heart is, I think she'll feel that and want to wait for you, too."

The pottery wheel spins and whirrs as my hands surround a small wet lump of clay. I press firmly, trying to keep the pressure even in order to center the gray mound before beginning to make an indentation in the center, then hollowing out the gray mass before carefully pulling up the sides of the pot. I have no idea what I'm making. I just concentrate on holding my hands steady and not letting the walls get too thin or uneven or else — *wonk wonk splat!* — the whole thing collapses and I have to start over.

I am hiding out in the ceramics shop that I've discovered on the base, having largely given up the expectation that wandering about I might make what Malwell calls "casual" therapeutic contacts. I thought I might meet some family members here and have conversations, but in fact I'm almost always alone. Provided with clay and some minimal instruction, I'm now free to play there whenever the shop is open. After some weeks of practice, I finally succeed in making two very small pots that I name "Paper Clip Pot" and "Ashtray," and have them fired. I'm proud of how they turned out. I choose a glaze and then paint some tiny bare winter trees on them as a memento of my stay here.

Did I mention the beautiful trees? As I drive around the base, I am captivated by the beauty of the intricate skeletal shapes of the large old trees that line every street. I've been taking photos, trying to capture their exquisite designs, every one different. I'm surprised by the mystery of finding so much beauty in the barren branches of trees whose names I do not know. One weekend, I take a drive out to the recreation area called Land Between the Lakes. More elegant trees, fields of golden grasses, and even a herd of bison. The sparse, subtle beauty feeds my soul, and I am grateful.

One day the Merks are invited to attend a session of an Army Family Team Building class. Caitlin, the 40-something, sturdy-looking Army spouse who is teaching it, has been several times around the block. She bluntly admits, "We have trouble getting people to come in for this training, so you might as well sit in." She has a wealth of information about how the Army operates as a social system, and her goal is to impart this to other spouses who are new to the Army, but she is happy to answer questions we may have.

"The Army preys upon naïve young people in getting them to

enlist," she says. "The recruiters stop just short of lying as they describe what the soldier can expect. One thing they seldom point out is that a four-year enlistment contract has a clause that for the four years *after* the enlistment ends, they can be called back if the Army needs them. What spouses need to understand is that the soldier is expected to believe that the Army comes first. I wish spouses didn't have to find this out the hard way, when they are upset about the long hours and the deployments. The upside? Well, there *is* free child care."

The business about recruiters lying is old news to me. It's one reason peace activists try to keep recruiters off high school campuses. But the reservist clause — I had no idea they were signing away that many years of their lives. It's especially chilling to hear this from an Army insider.

Caitlin strongly advises spouses who do not have jobs of their own to get involved in volunteer work to ward off depression, especially during deployments. Then she adds, "You probably didn't know that there are gang members in the Army. There is much more crime on the base than off, so most families decide to take their BAH (Basic Allowance for Housing) and live off-base."

A brief moment of silence as we try to take in this shocking statement.

"Gangs in the Army?" blurts a wide-eyed Merk.

"I kid you not. The FBI did a study in 2008 showing that 1-2 percent of military members have a gang connection. That's higher than the rate in the general population. Crips, Bloods, Aryan Brotherhood, MS-13. All of those and more. Some gangs encourage members to enlist to get weapons training and access to weapons."

"Can't the Army screen for that at recruitment?"

"They say they do. But the recruiters are under a lot of pressure to issue waivers for those with minor criminal offenses in order to keep up their numbers. And they don't really have enough training to spot the signs of gang membership."

Whoa. This is going to take some time to process. It's very scary that gangs are now using the Army as a training ground. After hearing all of this, one Merk asks Caitlin how she has coped with being an Army wife for so many years.

"I make it work for me. Once you understand that the Army talks out of both sides of its mouth, you know how to look for the truth. After a while, things get predictable and you know where you stand and how you can maneuver. I try to share what I've learned with spouses who are new to this."

THE NEXT WEEK DURING THE HOURS I'm assigned to one of the three Merk offices, I'm sitting doing crossword puzzles when a young Hispanic couple comes in.

"Is this the Military Coaches?" asks the woman. She's a little plump, wearing a neat knee-length black dress. Her husband is right behind, in his Army fatigues.

"That's right. Come on in, have a seat," I say, getting up to close the door behind them.

"We've been having some problems," she says shyly, eyes downcast. "We made an appointment to see the Family Life Chaplain, but it's not until two weeks. I didn't want to wait."

"I'm glad you reached out to the chaplain. They help a lot of people with marriage problems." I say this because I'm panicking, having had no training or experience in couples counseling. Usually I've managed to hand such cases off to another counselor, but now I'm trapped. "But it's fine you're here now, " I assure them, "so please, tell me what's going on."

Her husband is sitting slouched on a chair beside her, eyes glazed over. She gives him a fierce look, then sits up very straight and looks me in the eye.

"OK. I tell you what happen with him. He just came back from Iraq, this month. He's all the time on his computer after dinner, but I don't complain. He says it helps him relax, and I know he's stressed, very stressed. He has his own room, like an office, and that's where he goes. Last week ..." her voice catches. "Last week I want to show him something our son made at school, and I walk into the room. What do I see?" She tears up. "I don't think I can even say it. On the computer. Pictures. Women, men, I don't look even to see what they're doing. He's got his pants unzipped..." At this point she can no longer speak, but cries softly.

Her husband is making a study of the ceiling tiles, perhaps counting them. No one seems to know what to say, certainly not me.

"And the worst thing, the worst," she says, her voice increasingly like a growl, "the children were in the house. With the children in the house!"

He shifts in his chair, as though he might say something, but doesn't.

"What's wrong?" she cries. "We have sex every day, sometimes even twice. Aren't you satisfied with me?"

He finds his voice and reaches his hand tentatively toward her. "No, honey, you're fine. No, it's not you. I'm so sorry. It's just something we all did when we were downrange. I guess it got to be like a habit." She allows him to take her hand. "I'm so sorry," he says again. "I didn't mean to hurt you."

As they sit there quietly, I'm thinking, "Holy shit." Not only am I not a marital therapist, but I also have no background in sexual or online addictions. Where do we go from here? All I can do is trust my heart, which feels enormous sympathy for these young people whose relationship has been threatened by military service in a new, unexpected way. I'm flailing, and say something about compulsive behaviors being a way to reduce anxiety. That's probably not helpful. I help them talk so they might listen to each other's feelings, trying to shift the focus to the parts of their relationship that are actually working. I want them to put things in context. They grow calmer as we talk about the values they share, and what their marriage is about. Thank God they're going to see the chaplain.

IN THE BACKGROUND OF ALL OUR ASSIGNMENTS lurks Malwell, a shadowy, faceless entity that meets us primarily in cyberspace, and doles out information on a strict need-to-know basis. The corporation gives us our rules of engagement ("Stay in your lane") and issues our paychecks. I've already learned that I can expect my queries to be ignored. For example, when we'll be getting cell phones for an assignment, or when we will get another assignment. I've also heard whisperings from old-timers. "Don't complain about anything. They'll hold it against you. I know someone who got fired because she complained about her insane coworker." We Merks do our best to network and share information in private, mindful not to irritate the corporate ogre many of us imagine is waiting to attack us.

To keep us on a short leash, we're obliged to endure a group "supervision" call each week with other Merks on our base and someone at corporate headquarters. This set-up is something between absurd and humiliating, because the Merks typically have vastly more experience than the supervisor wielding this authority. We do a voice conference call, each of us calling in separately from our hotel room, which means we can't see each other. It might go like this.

"Good morning. Wilma here. How are y'all doin' today?"

A chorus murmurs "Fine."

"Good, good. I just want to go over this Duty-to-Warn protocol one more time. Have you got any questions before I do?"

Silence. We've heard this all before.

"Okay, well, just let me go over this." She drones on for ten minutes about the decision-making algorithm to be used in cases of persons experiencing or reporting abuse or being at risk of self-harm or harm to others . "So, any questions?"

Silence.

"Well then, that's fine. So tell me what it's like there, how you've been spending your time. Let's hear from … Maureen? What'cha been doin'?"

I'm expecting such a question so I've prepared a list. "I've met one plane, seen a couple of soldiers in the office, and I went to a meeting for spouses, the Info Exchange. Making the rounds, getting some casual contacts." I don't mention the ceramics studio.

"Well that's just fine. Someone else?"

"It's Diane. I have to say, we have just been having a fabulous time! Everyone is so wonderful here, and we've been really busy. This is a terrific base. It's a great assignment!"

I can't believe what I'm hearing. I know very well that we're so overstaffed that no one could be busy. The game is to while away time waiting for our brief stints of office time.

"Oh, yes, I agree. This is Arlene. There's *so* much to do. This is a really great opportunity for service! And like Diane says, the people are so friendly and helpful. It's such a *privilege* to work with the military."

It goes on like this, with a few others singing the praises of this assignment, and Wilma seems pleased. By the end of the call, I'm in a state of shock. Who are these people? What makes them shuck and jive like that? They seem to know what Malwell wants to hear, and they lay it on thick. Do they think this will help them get more assignments? Clearly, I am out of step. Should I be acting that way to keep my job? They must be made of different stuff than I, who struggles to sound productive without telling an outright lie. The hope that I will find pals, confidantes in this group grows dimmer. I'm disappointed not to be able to trust them.

The Merks tend not to talk politics openly, so I've been unable to determine if any of them is as excited about Obama's inauguration as I am. I decide not to leave my hotel room on January 20, keeping my phone handy in the unlikely event that someone wants to contact me. I settle in to watch the ceremony and the speeches, knowing my friends and political allies all over the country as are as joyful as I that this historic moment has arrived. And the balls! Watching Barack and Michelle dance with elegance is like a fairy tale come to life.

The next day I return to the base to read more books at Starbucks, but then a huge ice storm hits the South and I'm stuck at the hotel because the base is temporarily closed. I'm thrilled to remain in my room to cook and read more books, gazing out the window at the trees and bushes hung with fantastic pink-tinged icicles.

So far from home, out of my comfort zone, and with so little actual work to do, this assignment begins to feel like a spiritual retreat. There is no director, so I'm on my own with plenty of time to meditate and read the books I've brought. I review my notes from my October Buddhist retreat, and study what are called slogans, which are part of the Seven Points of Mind Training teachings, or *lojong*. I'm reading B. Alan Wallace's *Buddhism with an Attitude,* which offers explanations of these fifty-nine slogans. I focus on the one that says, "Transform adversity into the path of spiritual awakening." If I could make good use of the adversity I experience, rather than moan and complain, that would be life-changing.

I'm also taking a distance-learning course from the gentle lamas who have become my teachers, in which we practice the *tonglen* breathing meditation of "taking and sending." I think about how this could apply to my current situation, surrounded by people who risk their lives engaging in warfare. I go out for a walk one unseasonably warm February day, pondering the teaching that everything in life is impermanent. Halfway across the field adjacent to the hotel, I start breathing more consciously, doing the *tonglen* practice. Breathe in adversity, breathe out love. Breathe in the fact of warfare and killing, breathe out comfort to those immersed in those activities. Keep breathing. This gives me something to do in order not to feel completely helpless. It's hard for the hard-nosed, scientific side of me to believe that my prayers make a difference to others or to the state of the world, but the act of intentionally breathing and sending love does create some expansion and peace in my heart. I'll take that.

A question that continues to preoccupy me: What is the Army? I remain bewildered at the enormity of this phenomenon and the complexities and contradictions I observe. I find no place to stand where I can see the Army in its entirety, so I've been pondering the Buddhist idea that *nothing arises independently.* The Army is a set of components: the people, the materiel, the policies, the behaviors, the reputation. The Army depends for its existence on these constituent parts. Yet any of these might change or be replaced, and the Army would continue to exist. We speak of the Army as a real entity, but certainly it has no independent existence separate from its components, from my own journey or from the lives of countless other beings. I, too, seem to be a part of this constantly-changing set of circumstances. The Secretary of Defense has contracted with Malwell to bring in hundreds of us coaches, presumably hoping this will reduce domestic violence, suicide, and other forms of combat-related stress. But I find that there is little I can do to mitigate these large problems, which started way upstream. The violent arm of the Army has caused harm, and now the protective arm wants to stop the pain. It's a puzzle.

TOWARD THE END OF MY TIME AT FORT CAMPBELL, I wangle an invitation to meet informally with several wounded soldiers over lunch at the Fisher House. This is a large family-style residence where soldiers from other bases who are being treated at the Army hospital here can stay for brief periods with members of their family. These "warriors in transition" are willing to tell their stories of injury, protracted treatment, and disappointing recovery. They are still in the Army until it is determined whether they will recover sufficiently to return to duty, or will be discharged with a disability rating. One of them, a slight man with a head of dark brown hair not cut to military regulation, is clearly depressed and says he has had multiple psychiatric hospitalizations. I learn that he's had brain damage from a reaction to medication. When his wife hands him the baby, I notice how sweetly and gently he holds his infant son. I'm brimming with emotion when I leave this place, and go to sit quietly in my car and write.

in the atrium of hell
in the antechamber to war
a chord will not resolve
meanwhile
after medals are pinned and stories told
out the sly back door go the wounded
through the automatic doors and down the ramp
our heroes must make their own way
in a world where nobody knows
the trouble they've seen

THE MORE TIME I SPEND IN THE MILITARY ENVIRONMENT, the more I recognize that here the abnormal becomes normal. Spouses are gone for a year, home for a year, then gone again. People are being trained to kill. People get killed by being blown up. People witness horrible violence. It doesn't happen to everyone, but it's woven into the fabric of normal life in the military.

From the outside, my job appears to be an opportunity to offer comfort and support to my fellow humans and to accompany people in their trials. In fact, I've only rarely found a chance to do so, and have felt waves of anger and frustration about this. I fear I've been co-opted by the war machine and my presence here is actually a way of putting lipstick on the pig to make the Army look good. Yet despite my discomfort with military culture and my ambiguous role, I still hope that sooner or later I will bring my skills into practice. And perhaps I have learned lessons in patience, tolerance, kindness and self-recognition, and for that I leave feeling grateful. I'm also delighted to learn I will finally be sent to Fort Lewis next month, the base closest to where I live and the assignment I've repeatedly requested.

CHAPTER 6

FORT LEWIS DREAM

2009

Driving north on Interstate 5, while I listen to the soothing sound of Eckart Tolle reading *The Power of Now*, the evergreen trees get taller the farther north I go. I feel my face relax into a smile. I'm on my way to a four-week assignment at Fort Lewis, south of Seattle, said to be the most requested of all Army bases. After three weeks at home recovering from the culture shock of Fort Knox and Fort Campbell, I've reached some equanimity and peace of mind. Practicing the Tibetan Buddhist instruction to "regard all phenomena as dreams," I'm delighting in my life.

By evening, I've settled in the pleasant, quiet accommodation reserved for me near Fort Lewis, a furnished studio apartment with a sleeping loft. Over a light supper, I feel excited, wondering what this assignment will bring.

In the morning, I enter the enormous installation carved out of a forest just south of Tacoma. Huge cedar trees tower everywhere, and recreation areas on post include a lake with boating and camping available to anyone with a military connection. A number of acres have been completely cleared as an airfield where soldiers train to be the pilots and crew of Army helicopters.

A half-dozen Merks work out of the Army Community Services office. When I introduce myself on the first day, I learn that there are two offices designated for our use, and a schedule board to reserve them. Three of us have traveled some distance for this job and we are glad to be here. Those who live locally greet us tepidly. Before I arrived, a fellow Merk had warned me about the locals' resentment toward those whose travel expense and lodging are paid. When I report to the office one of the locals, a petite woman with dark hair, sits reading a magazine, our trademark gold plastic Merk nametag affixed to her sweater. I'm curious to learn whether she might be companionable.

"Hi, Francine," I say, glancing at her nametag. "How's your morning going?"

"Oh, just fine," she says without looking up.

"Anything I can help with?"

"I don't think so. It's all under control."

She continues reading, so I occupy myself scrutinizing bulletin boards, looking for useful information. I try again to engage her. "So you're from around here, right?"

She finally makes eye contact. "I live in Tacoma. I've had a bunch of rotations here. Malwell likes to assign people they don't have to pay housing for."

"I see. Still, I'm really glad to get this assignment, since there are no military bases near me in Oregon."

"The longer you work here, the more you get to know the players."

"I suppose that's true."

"Like the Base Commander. He's a great guy, and he likes our work. He doesn't understand why they keep bringing in people from out of the area. But I don't care, as long as I get to keep working here steady." She gets up. "Gotta make some phone calls." She goes into another room and shuts the door. Feeling dismissed, I leave the building and go for a walk.

Later that morning, I appear for our scheduled staff meeting. It will be run by Donna, the designated lead Merk and our liaison to the POC. My source told me she's another one who lives nearby and has been assigned here repeatedly. A heavyset woman in a print dress and cardigan sweater, she's on the phone looking away from me when I arrive, speaking in an authoritative tone. Francine comes in and nods to me. When Donna hangs up the phone I start to greet her, but she looks past me to smile at Francine.

"Hey, Francine. I think after the meeting I'll go over to the Chinese buffet for lunch. Want to come?"

"Oh great! I haven't been there in a while."

I can take a hint. They feel entitled to their jobs, I am a threat, and they choose to deal with this by ignoring me. But I'm so mellow I'm largely able to overlook this dynamic, especially knowing I'll be here only four weeks. I do envy their good fortune to have regular work, but I remind myself to be kind and not let their behavior bother me.

The beauty of the rainy Northwest is stunning. On rare clear days, Mt. Rainier looms in the near distance. After the culture shock of the German assignment and the peculiar discomfort of Southern military culture, this West Coast location feels much more like home. There's even an espresso shop called Battle Beans right in the building where I work.

At a welcoming event for newcomers to the base, I pick up a free insulated lunch sack with a bank logo on it, and a keychain with a flashlight from some other military-friendly organization. As people file past my table and glance at our brochures, one woman smiles, looks me in the eye, and says, "We're so grateful for your program. We got some good help with our marriage at Fort Hood."

The man beside her agrees. "You do a good service. Thank you."

Since I had no requests for service in Bamberg or Fort Knox and so few at Fort Campbell, I'm surprised but gratified to learn that sometimes our work has been helpful. The people who work here, both the service members and the civilians, seem more relaxed than those I met in Kentucky, as though part of their lives might take place outside of military culture.

For the first time I have regular work to do, and I'm pleased. A woman soldier calls for an appointment, and I'm able to see her the next day. She is in her twenties, tall and big-boned. She sits down heavily, with a sigh. I see her rank is specialist.

"My unit is deploying in three months," she blurts, "and I still don't have a Dependent Care Plan for my son. He's 18 months old. His father is a loser — I don't even know where he is."

"I'm sorry he's not here to help. But what about your family, is there anyone who could take him while you're gone?"

"My mother's in Virginia. She's an alcoholic and I can't leave him with her. My sister just lost her job and her husband is a bully. They can't take him. If I don't find a safe place for Ronnie before we deploy, I'll be discharged from the Army." Her eyes brim with tears. "I don't know what to do. I need this job to support him."

"Of course. Are there other relatives — grandparents? aunts?"

She shakes her head. "I've been thinking and thinking. I could be gone a year. There ain't nobody I can trust." She pauses to wipe her tears. "I used to be close to my dad but since I got pregnant, he's turned his back on me. He's super-religious. He hates I'm not married. We don't talk no more."

A single mom in the Army with virtually no family support. The Army will apparently not defer deployment in these circumstances, but instead cut the soldier loose. If she loses her Army job, the best she could hope for might be to live on welfare, and where would she go to live?

I shake my head in sympathy. "I'm so sorry to hear that. But you know, I think your unit chaplain would be a good person to talk with. That's part of their job, to help soldiers work out family problems related to Army expectations. He understands how the Army works, and could help you figure out what choices you have, short of leaving the Army."

"I don't know ... I don't know if anyone can help," she says, but takes the card I hand her. It's the best I have to offer. I hope the chaplain knows what to do.

A steady stream of requests for counseling come in. Though not busy all the time, I have enough work to gain an understanding of when soldiers and spouses will ask for help. A male soldier with two prior deployments tells me he's already experienced nine improvised explosive devices going off in his vicinity. He's got mild traumatic brain injury as a result. "I can't think as quick as I used to," he says. "Sometimes I get confused. I don't think the Army is taking it seriously. My captain said we should all expect to deploy again this year. I don't feel ready."

With each session, I develop more compassion for soldiers and their families, who often face unusual and painful challenges due to their military lifestyle. I begin to ask soldiers their reasons for choosing military service. Mostly these are imminently practical:

One specialist says, "Once we had our second child, there was no way we could support them on what we made. The Army gave me a job, housing, and health benefits."

"The judge said he'd dismiss my charges if I joined the military," says a wiry, heavily-tattooed young soldier. "Sounded like a good way to avoid jail."

Another says, "I want to go to college, but I can't afford it unless the Army pays for it. All I have to do is get through these three years."

A sign on the recruitment office door reads, "Wake up and smell the economy!" Economic survival is a powerful motivator.

Many soldiers also mention wanting to serve their country, but make little comment about the wars in Iraq and Afghanistan and whether or not these are worth fighting. Some will say frankly that they disagree with the reasons for starting the conflict, but remain willing to participate in what they hope will be a disengagement process.

"I have to get back to Iraq to support all our soldiers who are still there," says one staff sergeant. "Sooner or later, the Iraqis will be trained and strong enough to hold their own."

Another says, "We're trying to help with building clinics and schools in Afghanistan." Then he winces and adds, "Trouble is, the Taliban keeps blowing them up." Though the soldiers may be intrigued by the technical aspects of war, weaponry and battle tactics, I encounter no blood lust or hatred in their hearts.

When Charlie the lead Merk mentions that various commanders at this post have formed a study group to read Larry Dewey's *War and Redemption*, I check out a copy from the base library. A comprehensive overview of PTSD (called shell shock and battle fatigue in years past), it is written by a therapist who worked with American war veterans over a period of thirty years. The inevitability of these syndromes is what hits home. He speculates there was no less psychological injury in World War II than in Vietnam, but that it took longer for veterans to come forward and acknowledge their suffering. Many turned up in his office, in fact, when their memories were stimulated by the vivid television scenes of battles in Indochina in the 1960s and 1970s.

Apparently the Army is gearing up for the long haul, expecting to send personnel into unconventional, "asymmetrical" war situations in the Middle East and Central Asia (Afghanistan and the other ethnic "-stans") for some time to come. In the library's Military Science section, I look for what the Army intelligentsia is reading and thinking about the geopolitical trends. I find books on the rise of militant Islam in Central Asia in the context of a long history of invasions, dynasties, empires and bloody battles that have transferred power again and again to outside rulers. It's hard to take in and store all this information. I feel as though I'm trying to memorize the pattern of waves coming up on the shore, each one like but unlike the one before. I nourish a hope that the new Obama administration will somehow find a sane, viable strategy to bring peace and self-determination to that area of the world.

In the evenings, I have time to read books, ponder ultimate questions, and revel in my good fortune. The other Merks never do warm up, but on the weekends I'm free to travel, so I take a ferry from Anacortes to Orcas Island in the San Juans and spend two nights in that magical place. Blessed with fair weather unusual for the rainy season, I drive up into Moran State Park, then climb to the top of an overlook tower constructed by the CCC in the

1930s, where I can see other islands in every direction. On another weekend, I drive up the Olympic Peninsula to Port Townsend and spend the night in a historic hotel that is reputed to have once been a high-class brothel. I'm alone on both these weekends, yet feel somehow accompanied by the spirits I sense dwelling in these places, which gives me a strong sense of belonging here. I feel joyous and relaxed. On a third weekend, I'm treated to a tour of Seattle by my old friend Miriam who lives there, and we explore farmers' markets, warehouse clothing sales, and a Korean women's spa. I also find time to knock about Pike's Place Market and take the underground tour of the regions beneath Seattle. I almost feel embarrassed by how much fun I'm having.

Back at the base, I see a new client during my office hours. A slender white woman comes in, casually but stylishly dressed. Looking about thirty, she wears her blonde hair in a bob. Her face is pale and drawn. She sits on the edge of her chair.

"Is it true you don't keep records?"

"Yes, as long as you don't tell me you're on the verge of hurting yourself or someone else. I couldn't keep that confidential."

"No, no, nothing like that. I just need to talk about my marriage. My husband's deployed and is coming home in a month. He's a captain. The thing is, I don't feel like I'm in love with him anymore, and I think I need to tell him."

Uh-oh. This is what people say when they've met someone else. "What do you feel that makes you say you're not in love anymore?"

"When I think of him I just feel sort of blank. Like I don't miss him, and that doesn't seem right."

"How long have you been feeling this way?"

"Probably since soon after he left for Iraq last March. I got caught up in my job, which I really like, and I was relieved not to have him around wanting time with me. I felt more free."

"How long have you been married?"

"Four years."

"Children?"

"No."

"Has someone else entered the picture?"

"No, that's not it. I feel like something is missing, but I don't know what it is. Do you think I should tell him before he comes home?"

"Definitely not. He needs to stay focused on his job through the whole deployment. This is something you'll need to talk about in person." I still wonder if she's been talking to another man, but I won't press that. "Tell me more about you and your husband. When did you meet, and how?"

She finally settles back into the chair, and gives me a brief smile. "About four years ago we met through friends and started dating. I never thought I'd go for a military man, but he was such a gentleman! And straightforward, so it was easy to trust him. We started talking about marriage, and since he was due to be deployed in a few months, we decided to go ahead before he left. That time he was only gone six months, and when he got back, we finally started to get to know each other."

"And how did that go?"

"We had a few differences, but we were trying to work with them. Like what to spend money on, or how to decorate the house. Or even how to make decisions. He likes to do things spur-of-the-moment, and I like to plan. I realized I hadn't gotten to know him very well before we married, and his being away didn't help. I got a promotion at work and that meant I was working longer hours. Then he got deployed again, that time for almost a year. It was becoming a long-distance relationship, and not very satisfying."

"Did you talk about it when he came home?"

"Not really. We were just trying to have as good a time as we could before he was sent away again. And he did leave last March, this time to Iraq. I guess that's when I started thinking this is not the marriage I want to have."

"Okay, I'm getting the picture. You and your husband definitely need to talk. And you'll want a therapist who can help you both share your feelings about the marriage. Try to keep your mind open about the future. And mainly, try to be kind as well as honest with him."

"Thanks," she says, exhaling deeply. "It's good to get this off my chest. I'll look for a therapist we can see once he's home."

My assignment ends all too soon, and I wend my way back down Interstate 5 to Ashland. I reflect on how much better I feel, finally to have had therapeutic sessions with the clientele I'd come to serve. It was the chance to help others that I'd hoped for in this job. I've managed to secure a follow-on assignment at the end of June for six weeks at the Army War College in Pennsylvania, so now I have two months to simply relax at home.

CHAPTER 7

THE GUARD GOES TO WAR

The first weekend in May 2009, while I'm at home waiting to go to the War College, the corporation sends me to support a half-day Army ceremony at the Jackson County Fairgrounds just outside Medford. My local Army National Guard, the First Battalion of the 186th Infantry, is being mobilized to join the war in Iraq. This battalion includes companies from Ashland, Medford, Grants Pass, Roseburg, and Coos Bay. When I show up, the group from Roseburg is just arriving in buses, escorted by veterans on motorcycles. The bikers are passionate about bearing witness to the service of these soldiers and supporting the families they leave behind. They hand out wristbands that say "Support Our Troops."

The day is rainy and cool and the covered horse arena is cavernous and drafty. I arrive about an hour early and observe as family members and friends in jackets and heavy sweatshirts find seats in the bleachers. Most are women and children. I've been asked to support this event, but what does that mean? People are huddled in small groups. It would seem rude to elbow my way in to such a group and ask how they are feeling. I'm wearing my badge but no one is noticing me. I try sitting in several different spots, hoping I might catch someone's eye and ask whom they know who is deploying. I overhear snatches of conversation, but nothing I can imagine breaking into. This is a solemn moment, and I am loath to be intrusive.

I spot a tall, lanky soldier standing alone, with one foot pushing back against a thick column supporting the arena's roof. I approach him, note his sergeant's stripes, and ask if he, too is being deployed.

"No, not this time," he says. "I'm part of the rear detachment, staying behind."

He tells me this group is headed first to Georgia for special training, then to Iraq, where their job will be "reconnaissance and security." At this point in the war, the U.S. is trying to hand off combat duties to the Iraqi National Army.

"So how dangerous do you think that will be?"

"You never know. I expect most of them to come back, but not for a year. It's tough on the families."

Especially Guard families, I think. Unlike regular Army, they often live in towns where most people have no military connection. Neighbors may have no idea about the stresses of deployment or that the families need support. Since 2003, Guard soldiers are no longer the "weekend warriors" deployed only for disaster assistance or civil unrest. Now they are called up to fight wars.

The building brims with the expectancy and resignation of the supporters crowding in. The mood is somber. I see one female soldier carrying an infant and something inside me twists up. A mother with an infant. *Oh, please, don't make her go!*

Five hundred soldiers march in formation onto the dirt floor of the arena, to the music of a small group from the Army Band. They are wearing the rumpled camouflage outfits that always remind me of children's pajamas, and their pant legs are tucked into desert boots. They do not look the least bit ferocious, and some look scarcely tall enough to be soldiers. Surely these young people are not meant to fight a war? They stand at parade rest, hands behind their backs, throughout a lengthy program which begins with a few tunes by the Southern Oregon Scottish Bagpipe Band and the ceremonial exchange of flags and banners.

Then the speeches begin with Governor Kulongoski promising to ensure that the Guard's needs for equipment and supplies are met, and to see that families are supported in their absence. He vows, "We will watch your back." Senators Wyden and Merkley are in Washington, D.C. on this day, but send prepared remarks to be read by others. Mayor Stromberg of Ashland makes an impromptu speech. It sounds as though he hasn't been involved with the Guard's business previously, but he promises to keep track of their movements from this point forward. The promise makes it plain that the war only seems far away if we don't recognize that our neighbors are among those doing the fighting. But I also wonder, is there a plan, a strategy, an achievable outcome? The scene is timeless, archetypal, human, and sad. I wonder what will become of them, or those of us who care for them.

For the rest of the month I'm happy to put aside all thoughts of the military and enjoy my semi-retired, overprivileged life in the peaceful vacation destination of Ashland. I kayak on the lake, take improvisational dance classes, and sing with a women's choral group. I do yoga, make collages, shop at the farmers' market, and have lunch with friends. I work in my garden and meditate at the local Buddhist temple. I browse an online dating site. Some days I revel in doing nothing at all.

I take a one-week road trip to California to visit all my relatives. My mother is eighty-seven now, and her memory is falling away more and more. I'm saying good-bye to my childhood home of southern California, leaning in to the strangeness of working for the military. The military is said to be fighting wars on our behalf to preserve the American way of life. Yet I know our consumer culture is unsustainable and all of us, myself included, ought not to feel entitled to our wasteful ways.

On the drive home, I take a break at Gaviota Beach and look out into the gleaming Pacific Ocean, saying a silent prayer.

May I be an instrument of peace. May I radiate love to all who cross my path. May I be strong and calm in the tumultuous times now unfolding. I give thanks for my life, and may my life be of benefit to the larger whole. Blessed be this planet and this universe.

Then I have four days to tie down the flaps on my Ashland life, get one last massage, and pack for my next six-week trip which will be to Carlisle, Pennsylvania, home of the U.S. Army War College. Yikes.

CHAPTER 8

FIREFLIES AT THE WAR COLLEGE

2009

A Buddhist teaching by Jack Kornfield goes through my head while I'm sitting in the Medford airport. "Do not seek perfection in a changing world. Instead, perfect your love." If only I could always remember to do that. This morning it seems almost possible. The shuttle driver was friendly. My bag was a tad overweight and the airline person let it pass. The coffee shop waitress gave me extra cream. TSA did not hassle me. As our plane taxis into position, the yellow wildflowers carpeting the grassy median between runways make me smile.

A few hours later, we land in Chicago. Now it's a four-hour wait at O'Hare for the next plane to Harrisburg, Pennsylvania. I wander through the C Concourse in search of a quiet place to rest. There is no such place. The smell of pepperoni pizza and popcorn is everywhere, and the din is fantastic. Everyone is either shouting to a travel companion or hollering into a cell phone. Unintelligible announcements rumble out about flights being changed and the constant reminders that we are at "Threat Level Orange." An outer circle of Hell, I think. Defiant, I walk about singing, "Why have we come to earth? To serve, and remember to love." I am gently amused by praying aloud while no one pays me any mind. I sit down near a Starbucks and turn to the woman seated beside me. I ask what she thinks Threat Level Orange means. She looks at me with alarm and does not respond.

Then the United flight is delayed, so by the time I arrive in Harrisburg and collect my rental car, it is night. Somehow I find my way to the Residence Inn in Carlisle, where I'll stay for the next six weeks for my War College assignment. This is a high-level Army training facility for officers at the lieutenant colonel and colonel level who are being groomed to become generals. They will then take jobs at the Pentagon and other strategic positions in national security and international alliance organizations. Students in this ten-month program also include officers from other branches of the military, civilian national security professionals, and officers in the militaries of U.S. allies. I'll be the only Merk at the installation, and I'm eager to establish myself as the competent counselor I know I am, and to integrate myself into the worklife of this place. I requested this assignment to get closer to the heart of the war machine. I imagine myself an investigative journalist, peering into the workings of the military.

The next morning, I locate the Army Community Services office on the ground level of a two-story brick building. No one sits at the reception desk, nor do I see papers, clothing, or coffee pot that would indicate anyone was working here today. I venture past the desk into a corridor, passing two empty offices before I encounter someone in the third. A middle-aged white woman in pants and a light zip-up sweatshirt is staring into her computer screen.

I poke my head in and smile. "Good morning. I'm Maureen, the new Merk."

She doesn't respond immediately, then grunts and gestures vaguely toward the corridor. "You'll want to talk to Ron, your predecessor, in the office on the end." She turns back to her computer. Two offices further down I find a skinny white man with collar-length dark thinning hair and a beard, sitting behind a desk and gazing into his laptop. As he peers at me over the top of his glasses, I note his hollow cheeks, and the drooping bags under his eyes.

"Hi, I'm Maureen, the new Merk," I call from the doorway.

Looking me up and down, he says, "Oh, yeah. That's right. I thought I might see you today." He seems engaged with his computer, so I wait a beat and then venture to sit in a chair opposite the desk. He continues his vacant stare into the laptop.

Apparently it's up to me to get the ball rolling. "So this is the office we use?"

"Yeah, this is it."

"How's it been going? Have you been busy?"

"Somewhat."

After another pause, I ask, "So where're you from, Ron?"

"Philly. I'm driving home tonight. Tomorrow's officially my last day, but Emily said it was okay to leave early. There's not much going on right now. There won't be any students until the new class comes in August."

No students. Did I hear this right? The officers I'm eager to meet won't even be on campus until I'm ready to leave?

"Well then, have there been staff wanting to talk with you?"

He shrugs. "Most of them are out on vacation. It's summer, and not much for them to do."

Do I detect irritation that I'm distracting him from whatever he's doing on the computer? I get curious, stand up and walk around to the side of his desk where I can see the screen. It reveals a chess board. An angry heat rises in my chest. "You're playing chess?"

He looks at me impassively. "Multitasking."

I have no future with this man, thankfully, so why bother to share my feelings? I step away from the desk. "Okay. So where would I find the ACS Director?"

"That's Emily. She's out at a meeting right now. You might find her later this afternoon. First office as you come in the front door."

"Got it. How about I just park my briefcase here while I go outside and take a look around?"

"Whatever."

I retrace my steps down the corridor, past the lone worker hunched over her computer, and escape into the June sunshine. I sit on a bench under a dogwood tree to process this new information: the War College is on summer break. There are no students on campus, and most of the faculty and support staff are on vacation. My dream of helping future generals get in touch with their hearts is fading fast. Once again, it seems that my presence is pointless. Even so, I'm still feeling peaceful. I'm well-fed and well-housed. There will apparently be few demands or expectations. I listen to the singing of the birds.

After lunch, the Director is in, a slender white woman in a nondescript white blouse sitting behind a large desk. I tap on the open door to get her attention. "Hello, I'm Maureen," I begin. I tell myself that the sour look on her face certainly has nothing to do with me.

"Oh, yes, the new Merk. Ron told me you'd been in. Come, have a seat. You're from where, now?"

"Oregon. Just got in last night."

"I guess you found the Merk office. I'd give you a tour, but hardly anyone's here right now. I'll show you the break room. It's got a refrigerator if you bring your lunch in." As she stands up, I see she's a head taller than I, and her khaki skirt is as nondescript as her blouse. Maybe she's Amish or something?

Back in her office after our tour of the refrigerator, she tells me I'm expected to attend a meeting tomorrow with the Command Group.

"The garrison commander Colonel Simms always likes to meet the Merks. It will be in his office, 9 sharp. The deputy commander will be there too. Come here before that and I'll take you over. Oh, and here's the Merk phone," she says, handing me the small standard-issue flip phone. "Ron had to leave early."

Our meeting ends as she turns back to her work. She's given me no guidance as to how I might make myself useful, and she still has not cracked a smile.

In the morning we go to the colonel's office. Two women sit with him around a large conference table. He's in the rumpled camouflage they all wear, whatever their rank. Black curly hair that barely meets the military standards for length frames his face, and his dark eyes twinkle beneath adorable long lashes.

"Welcome to the War College," he says, beaming at me. "So glad you could come and spend time with us. I won't be here long, though, just getting ready to hand it all off to another commander. Gotta blow this popsicle stand." He chuckles, looking pleased. "Here, this is the deputy commander, Arlene Jones," he goes on, gesturing toward the petite elderly woman seated to his right, who wears her platinum-blonde hair very short and swept up away from her face. Her sleeveless blouse displays strong, tanned arms. She nods and gives me a perfunctory smile. "And this here is Mrs. Brown, the head of MWR." That Morale, Welfare, and Recreation position would make her Emily's boss, I think, and Arlene would be the boss of Mrs. Brown. I want to understand the power dynamics here. Will any of these people be my ally?

"Very glad to meet you," Mrs. Brown says with a smile, standing up and offering her hand. She is slender and pale, with long dark brown hair. "Please, have a seat."

"Thanks Gert," Emily says to her. "Good morning, colonel." She glances at Deputy Commander Jones, who looks away as we sit down. Why does she avoid eye contact with Emily?

"Yes, we're all going to miss Colonel Simms," says the deputy. "There's a farewell lunch for him tomorrow outside at the golf course. I'm sure Emily will give you the details."

"Oh, do come," chirps Mrs. Brown. "MWR has organized it all. There'll be pizza and grilled sausages. It will be fun."

"A bus at the ACS building at 11 will take people down to the Pavilion," says Emily.

"Thanks. I'd like to go." I decide to engage the colonel to ask my burning question. "So I understand we're in a break between sessions — no students right now?"

The Colonel nods and begins to speak when Deputy Arlene jumps in. "Oh, you know, you're actually lucky. Some of the students can be so pompous," she says with a sniff. "But I'm sure you'll have plenty to do. Your predecessor was very busy. He was able to counsel people as he played golf with them."

I take a quick glance at people's faces around the table to see if this was a snide remark. Apparently not. He must have turned in burgeoning Activity Reports counting all those people he "counseled," and she accepted that as evidence of his productivity.

"Do you like to golf?" asks the colonel, hopefully. This is a test I'm doomed to fail.

"No, I'm not a golfer."

"Pity," he says. "It's really relaxing."

The pleasantries continue, with the colonel and his deputy both holding forth. I begin to wonder whom they're trying to impress with their little speeches. Surely it can't be me. My only role seems to be to nod and smile and agree with whatever is said. By the end of the meeting I've concluded that Emily and the deputy despise each other, but I couldn't say why. And my tenure here will be so short that I don't need or want to know.

The next day, I dutifully board the bus that carries a group of civilians a three-minute ride to the golf course. I can make little sense of the conversations around me on the bus, but the tone of judgment and complaint is unmistakable. I try to speak to my seat mate but I am ignored. I practice breathing in the suffering, breathing out peaceful presence. At the picnic, continued attempts at conversations fall flat until I approach a middle-aged white woman sitting alone.

"May I join you?"

"Certainly!" She smiles, and just getting a smile feels like a victory. We eat our sausages and listen together to the "roasting" of the commander and see him receive the customary framed certificates of appreciation.

I decline the return bus ride and stroll back to the ACS building. The lone worker is once again alone, today wearing a powder blue sweatshirt, and I decide to introduce myself. After all, I need to report a number of daily "contacts." Her name is Marla, and I ask her about her job.

"I think I've got about five different jobs now," she laments.

"Wanda's out sick, and Cal is just never around. I've got to get all this paperwork sorted out." She scowls at the piles of paper heaped on the floor surrounding her. "Too busy. Too much to do."

"I won't bother you then. But if you want me, I'll be in the Merk office."

She nods, grumbling under her breath.

Sitting at the Merk desk in this half-deserted building, I review how I'll occupy myself through six weeks of solitude. There's the pool and a gym with a class on "lumbar stabilization." I've brought Buddhist books and plan to do some meditation. I study a map for weekend road trips. There will be plenty of time for journaling. But what about the expectation that I will be "very busy" as Ron was seen to be? I suspect he had the same amount of nothing to do.

I spend a lot of time at the beautiful outdoor pool, swimming or reading in a lounge chair, and include any interchanges there on my activity report. A retired general's wife shares about the spy novel she's reading while her husband is off golfing with an old friend. A food service worker is arranging stools around the outdoor tiki bar. "Come back at 5 for happy hour," she suggests. Every day I take a stroll around the small campus and faculty housing area. If the deputy commander spots me as she zooms by in her golf cart, she'll at least see I'm showing up to work.

Whenever I walk by Marla's office she's sitting at the computer in one of her collection of pastel-colored zip-up sweatshirts, and the piles of paper are still on the floor. I begin to think that this is a sort of stage set, in which she makes herself appear to be busy when actually she's got little to do, just like me. I only catch a glimpse of her coworker Cal when he breezes into ACS from time to time, and never really grasp what his job is either.

Wanda finally returns from sick leave. She's an imposing figure, a tall dark Black woman with short straightened hair and an intense gaze. She eyes me warily. "Another Merk. Wow, you guys don't stay long."

"It's true, just six weeks."

"Well, I don't know how you get to trust someone in that short a time. But hey, no one asked me."

"I agree, it's definitely too short." She looks at me uneasily and moves away down the corridor.

After a week of getting the cold shoulder from the ACS staff, I begin to feel depressed. The most I get are some glum remarks about how much work they have to do, and they have no suggestions as to how I might make myself useful. Do they all hate their jobs? There is a pervasive odor of unhappiness in this building. I know I've done nothing to merit being so pointedly ignored, and try not to take it personally, but it hurts.

Ah, well. The air is warm and moist and wildflowers abound along the roadsides. The fields are tall with ripening corn. Amish ladies in old-fashioned dresses with doily-like cotton caps sell me cucumbers, tomatoes and blueberries at a roadside stand, their wagon pulled off to the side of the road. I'm completely extraneous here. I float on the surface like a water bug.

THE ENTRANCE TO THE WAR COLLEGE LIBRARY at the far end of Root Hall is wide and welcoming. Daylight filters through skylights, illuminating a large seating area with comfortable chairs upholstered in cobalt blue. I wander into the rows upon rows of open stacks, noting books catalogued by subject matter: Military History, Doctrine and Strategy, Leadership and Command, Psychology, Ethics, Law, Regional Studies. These holdings are far more vast than anything I've encountered previously in base libraries; here, war itself is a scholarly subject. A reading stand holds an open notebook listing course requirements and recommended books for the students, and the double-starred title, *On War*, by Carl von Clausewitz jumps out at me. I want to understand the nature of this military enterprise on a deeper level, so I find a copy in the stacks and settle into the comfortable reading room, musing that not only is it possible to study war, but people are actively doing it in this clean, well-lighted place.

Von Clausewitz, it turns out, was a nineteenth-century Prussian general who fought in the Napoleonic wars. His philosophical treatise considers war as a socio-political phenomenon, rather than an art or a science in itself, hence his famous statement, "War is the continuation of politics by different means." Not only does war violently force one party's will upon the other, but it also serves to solidify at home the abstract ideas for which lives were sacrificed. This weighty volume also mentions two other theories of war besides the political: the eschatological (war leads to fated, final outcome such as crusades, jihad, Manifest Destiny and Nazi Master Race), and the cataclysmic view of war as a human catastrophe, benefitting no one, which undergirds peace research and conflict resolution. I begin to see why it might take a college to study the history and theory of war.

This collection also includes a DVD, *The War Tapes*, in which filmmaker Deborah Scranton provided video cameras to three enlisted members of a National Guard Infantry unit from New Hampshire on their way to Iraq in 2003. She encouraged them to keep written journals and stayed in contact with them during their tour.

In this film, two of the three cameramen are nominally supportive of the mission, but strive to show the awfulness and complexity of their daily situation and the dilemmas they face in an insurgency where the enemy may be in civilian garb. "I killed a child," says one soldier. "I'm a father. I'm afraid to tell my wife. She'll think I'm a monster." They share the view that the defense contractor KBR (Kellogg Brown & Root), whose truck convoys these soldiers are tasked to defend, is making scandalous amounts of money providing daily logistical support to the troops.

The third soldier admits privately that he is opposed to the war, seeing it as a thinly-veiled grab for Middle Eastern oil, yet his passion for his career leads him to say, "I love being a soldier. The only bad thing about the Army is you can't pick your war." This striking statement helps me better understand the soldiers' memoirs I have read. The career soldier's identity has little to do with politics and everything to do with pride and devotion.

I'm surprised to find such provocative material in the War College's collection. Perhaps this shows that military leadership does not shy away from obvious contradictions and controversies and is also willing to pay attention to soldiers' lived experience. Yet the idea of war as an unthinkable catastrophe is clearly not the emphasis in this setting.

There's one building where I'm not allowed access. I'm told it's where computer experts spend all year tweaking programs for war games which the students engage in during a two-week period. Various scenarios can be simulated and virtual warfare practiced. To my surprise, some hypothetical examples are detailed openly on the College's website for anyone to ponder. The one that sticks with me is a surprising one — the Mexican government collapses and we have a failed state on our southern border. I admit I'm glad that someone has taken the time to contemplate such a possibility, in order to be better prepared in an emergency. And again I'm impressed with the military's willingness to be open about its *raison d'être*, contrasted with defense contractor Malwell's secretiveness and obscuration of its profit motive.

Gettysburg National Military Park is only thirty miles from the War College, so on the Fourth of July weekend I take a drive. The Park covers 6,000 acres of fields, orchards and woodlands surrounding the town of Gettysburg, where Union and Confederate soldiers fought a fierce, decisive, and costly battle over three days in July 1863. I had no idea the battleground would be so vast that I'd have to use my car in order to visit the various sections. The grass glows a vivid green on the gently rolling hills, and tiny white wildflowers peek out along the sides of the road. I park the car and climb a grassy slope to read the inscriptions on some of the hundreds of stone monuments scattered across several square miles. Each one honors a unit of soldiers who fought here, most dedicated to Northern regiments, but some erected to honor Southern soldiers. Twenty-seventh Connecticut Infantry. Maine Volunteers Company D. Eighth Illinois Cavalry. Some markers declare how many died in the field and how many died of their injuries. Forty to fifty thousand are thought to have been killed or wounded in this bloody battle.

The National Cemetery memorializes the Union soldiers and the Union victory. No Confederate soldiers were given burial here. Different regiments from Maryland fought on opposite sides in the war and thus here at Gettysburg as well, facing each other directly at the skirmish on Culp's Hill. A monument erected by the State of Maryland depicts a Union soldier and a Confederate soldier helping each other stagger off the battlefield. The artist has captured in bronze the haunted expressions on their lean, haggard faces. Standing before these men frozen in time, I absorb deeply the dire truth that not long ago, Americans fought each other to the death on this ground. An unhealed wound gapes open at this place.

Meanwhile, the town teems with shameless commerce. Not only souvenir shops and stores selling re-enactment props, but even a wax museum. A double-decker tour bus goes by, with large Americans spilling out the sides, headphones clamped over their ears. The enormous inscription on the bus: "Battlefield Tours. Dramatized in Stereo." My wish is that they will also have a chance to walk this ground and feel the vibration of mourning in the soil. I wonder — is the pain, the grief, the devastation of war something that is studied at the War College?

All the while, my foot pain has been building. It started back in Germany when I did all that walking in summer sandals. A podiatrist diagnoses plantar fasciitis and fits me with orthotic inserts. A specialty shoe store sells me a really ugly pair of white, wide-bottomed cross-trainer shoes to put them in. The foot feels better, but then I trip over my own feet walking outside at the hotel and crash onto the concrete sidewalk. When I can't get up immediately, the hotel calls an ambulance. No broken bones, but movement is so painful for a few days afterward that I use some of the narcotics prescribed at urgent care. The incident triggers another of my mournful inner rants on my general decrepitude, questioning whether I'm entirely fit for this job — and if it's obvious to everyone but me that I'm an old woman now.

Continuing my study of war, I take a weekend to visit Washington, D.C. There was no time for sightseeing when I marched to protest the Vietnam War as a student in 1967, and this is my chance to finally see some of the museums and monuments. I arrange to stay with a Unitarian couple in Arlington, Virginia, who rent out a basement room as a B&B to raise funds for their church. It's an old home in a tree-lined neighborhood, and Greta meets me at the door. She's tall and thin, with her dark hair artfully pulled back and swept up on top of her head. Elegantly attired in black pants, white silk blouse, and dangling gold earrings, she shows me my room which has a distinct damp basement odor. She also invites me to find space in their overflowing refrigerator for the gluten-free food I've brought with me.

She introduces her husband, who's tall and lanky in his tweed jacket. "Will you join us for a glass of wine?" she asks. "Michael and I picked up a couple bottles of an excellent Merlot at the Barbourville winery last week. We can't wait to share it." She points to the living room where she and her husband are entertaining another couple. "These are our friends Ted and Lila." The man gets halfway out of his seat to greet me before deciding to sit down again. I feel scruffy in my jeans and sweatshirt. The term "Washington power couple" floats through my mind.

"Thanks, but no, I'm not much of a wine drinker." Her face freezes. Who is this uncivilized person she has allowed into her house? Feeling paranoid, I excuse myself and retreat to the basement, remembering the reason I'm here — their place is ideally situated near a Metro stop. I can catch a train into the city and spend two full days exploring the nation's capital.

In the morning, my first stop is the National Museum of the American Indian. The exterior's sweeping lines and curving surfaces are covered with natural limestone blocks, and the building is surrounded by flowing water rushing through small waterfalls.

Inside the entrance, an atrium is open five stories to the top of the building. I ascend steps to view the numerous exhibition rooms.

There is a peaceful feeling here. The corridors are dimly lit, but inside display cases are lighted objects from dozens of Native American cultures, including sculpture, wood carvings, tools, ceramics, ceremonial objects, clothing and jewelry collected over years by anthropologists or donated by the tribes themselves. The entire scope of the Americas is represented, from the Amazon to the Arctic and all the woodlands and deserts in between.

The museum both celebrates and memorializes these cultures, most of which have been all but obliterated in the years since Europeans came and conquered. The tragic tales of broken treaties, displacement, and slaughter are told. White men coveted Indian lands in Georgia, Alabama, Florida, Tennessee and North Carolina, and over a period of years in the 1830s, tens of thousands of people were forcibly removed to land that is now Oklahoma, many dying on the journey now known as the Trail of Tears. The role of the U.S. Army cavalry in then driving the Plains Indians from their lands is covered only minimally, with a reference instead to "the courageous warriors who fought to defend their nations in the 1879s and 1880s." Subsequently, the children of the remaining dislocated Indians were packed off to Christian boarding schools to learn English and forget their native ways. Yet the curation of the museum has chosen to emphasize the ways these societies flourished for hundreds of years rather than on their tragic diminishment and demise.

I softly speak tribal names, hearing the haunting music they evoke: Inca, Quechua, Maya, Yaqui. Paiute, Dine, Pawnee, Kiowa. Choctaw, Mi'kmaq, Potowatomi, Inuit. Offering a prayer for these strong, diverse peoples and lost cultures, I break away for lunch in the museum's cafeteria, where traditional foods from these tribes are offered, interpreted by a gourmet chef.

Then I seek out the United States Holocaust Memorial Museum. The permanent exhibition begins on the third floor and descends through a series of rooms chronicling the rise of Nazism in Germany through photos, video footage and artifacts. Quietly and powerfully, the story is told of anti-Semitic propaganda, theories of racial purity, violence against Jews and the rapid eroding of their status, through the culmination in the horror of the extermination camps. We are solemn and respectful as we walk through an entire room of shoes discarded by people about to enter gas chambers. The story of Hannah Senesh rivets me: a Jewish woman executed at the age of 22 after parachuting into the territory behind German lines in an attempt to rescue Hungarian Jews headed for the death camps. She wrote this poem, displayed in one of the final rooms as I leave the museum:

Blessed is the match consumed in kindling flame.
Blessed is the flame that burns in the secret vastness of the heart.
Blessed is the heart with strength to stop its beating for honor's sake.
Blessed is the match consumed in kindling flame.

AT DAY'S END MY BRAIN IS TIRED AND MY FEET SORE. Why not treat myself to a drink at the fancy 701 Restaurant on Pennsylvania Avenue? Thus a weary, unescorted woman of a certain age, in sneakers and carrying a daypack, walks into a bar. I ask to sit at a small table, and after a moment of hesitation, the host agrees. For a while I'm ignored, but finally a waiter in black shirt and spotless white apron appears and asks what I'd like. "Gin and tonic, please," I say. He nods, unsmiling, and disappears. Then another lengthy wait amidst the glass mirrors, crystal, dark walls and track lighting before I am served the drink. I'm surprised it comes in such a small juice glass, but I nurse it as long as I can, getting just a touch of relaxation and comfort for my aches and pains. I ask for the check, and pay three times the amount I've ever been charged for a drink in a bar before. On my way out the door I feel a smile forming: I don't really care.

When I return Sunday on the Metro, the day comes with bright blue skies, ice cream vendors everywhere, and people playing games on the grass. Flags ring the Washington Monument, flapping in the stiff breeze. The dome of the Capitol building is surrounded by scaffolding, and beside it, an enormous orange crane. Good. That Congress needs some work. Along the long black, reflective stone wall of the Vietnam Memorial, I pause to remember that time and that conflict, where so many of my generation died in a cause few can now defend. The bronze sculpture of Army nurses and a dying soldier is also poignant. I'm distressed to see a child clambering all over it with parents nowhere in sight. What can I say? The child has no idea what is represented here. I cannot find the words to teach him.

The classic lines of the World War II Memorial evoke a sense of peace. Understated grey stone pillars surround a blue fountain, and the sight of the flowing water seems to fill my heart with love for my father, a veteran of that war. Sitting in the shade on a stone ledge, I ponder my attitude toward patriotism over my lifetime. As a young child I was stirred by the Pledge's assertion of "liberty and justice for all." As a Girl Scout, I learned to raise and lower the flag and fold it carefully into triangles, keeping it from touching the ground. Still a Senior Scout when the Vietnam war began, in college I learned how imperfect and hypocritical our nation's behavior can be, and felt embarrassed and even ashamed to be American when travelling in Europe. Excessive flag-waving alarmed me, as did the mindless jingoism of people dangerously idolizing such symbols. Refusing to fly the flag or salute it became a protest against such nationalism. As a citizen of the world, I was happy to fly the Earth flag with its image of the planet as a whole.

When seeing the stars and stripes wave on military bases though, I've started to understand that soldiers take inspiration from this symbol of that for which they risk their lives. Here among all the memorials on the Mall, I can't help but feel grateful to those Union soldiers who "gave their lives that the nation might live." And to the GIs of my father's Greatest Generation, whose courage and sacrifice saved Europe from Hitler's tyranny. Working with the military has shown me another layer of life stress unfamiliar to most civilians. It has to do with the agreement to fight, kill, and even die following the orders of their leaders. They volunteer for this duty, and necessarily must believe their orders are legitimate. Coming as I do from a counterculture that encourages people to question authority, it is a struggle to understand how a person makes this choice. I may feel out of place in military circles, yet how can I not respect their values of honor, loyalty, and leadership? It's hard to hold both the dangers of militarism and the devotion of soldiers in mind at the same time. It's a paradox.

Drenched in history and now secretly proud to be an American, I return to Carlisle for my final week at the college. Students are starting to arrive for the next academic year, and the Merk office is one of the stops on their orientation tour. I am excited to have a chance to meet and greet each new colonel and lieutenant colonel. Since they are commanders of military units around the world, I'm keen to tell them about our confidential counseling program. I manage to engage each of them in a two-minute conversation and try to discover what their expectations are for the coming year. Some are tense, in full military regalia, and others stroll by in Bermuda shorts with families in tow. Some are gruff, others are relaxed and friendly. I gather that some are ambitious to work at the Pentagon, but others are pleased just to have a year off from command responsibilities. The National Guard officers are the most relaxed and approachable.

Late one afternoon, my phone startles me by actually ringing. It's a lieutenant colonel I'd spoken to earlier. He and his wife want to see me. I'm thrilled to be asked, and meet them the next day. She's a short, middle-aged fair-skinned woman, just a little plump, with her dark brown hair in a bob. Her husband is an inch or two taller, and wears khaki slacks and a muted plaid sports shirt.

"We'd like your help in talking something over," says the woman.

"Sure. What's the issue?"

The wife looks at her husband, who is looking out the window. Then they launch into a conversation that goes something like this:

"He's thinking of inviting my mother to live with us."

A brief silence, then he turns to me to explain, "Peg's dad died last year, and now her mom is alone."

"Yes, Mom's on her own now. But I think she's doing OK."

"She would never ask, you know. But I bet she's lonely."

"Chuck, that is so sweet of you to think of her. Really."

"She's such a lovely person."

"She is a lovely person, that's true. Lovely, but not lonely."

"How do you know?"

"We talk all the time! She's grieving my dad for sure, but you know, she has a life there in her little town, she has friends."

"And her health isn't the best."

"She's been cancer-free for five years. She's doing well."

"She's getting frail. She needs someone to look after her."

"Chuck, what is this about? Ronnie's away in college now, and Mary's off finding herself in Europe. Are you the one who's lonely?"

"No, of course not. I have you."

She hesitates, then says gently, "Are you missing your mom?"

He looks out the window again.

She explains to me, "His father died ten years ago, and his mother got ill."

"We were moving around so often, we couldn't offer her a place in our home."

"Your sister couldn't take her, either."

His voice gets shaky. "She ended up in a … facility."

Peg reaches for her husband's hand. He's breathing slowly, deliberately. No one says anything for a bit.

Peg muses softly, "She was a lovely person, too."

His eyes brim. He puts his other hand atop hers and gives a squeeze.

"Yeah. I do wish I could have done more."

"You did all you could. She's at peace now."

Another pause.

"You really think your mom will be okay?"

"For now, she's just fine. She wouldn't want to lose her independence."

"I suppose."

"Down the road, we'll see. Things could happen. We'll take it as it comes."

They're smiling now. They shift in their chairs, and start to stand up.

"Oh, this has been so helpful!" says Peg. "I can't thank you enough." Chuck gives me a warm handshake.

"So happy I could help." I see them to the door, tenderness in my heart as they walk away down the corridor, heads close together, talking softly.

ON THE LAST WEEKEND OF MY STAY, the Harrisburg Symphony gives a free public concert in a downtown Carlisle park. It's warm, early evening, and everyone's in shorts and sandals. People are wandering about licking ice cream cones. Families have brought lawn chairs, while some relax on blankets. I find a spot to sit on the border of a flower bed and soak in the peaceable energy. Suddenly a glowing green light appears a few inches from my face. As I focus my eyes, I gasp. An insect whose bottom is a green lantern flutters its wings before me. My first firefly, at age 59! I feel the delight of a five-year-old. I'm grinning, watching them come and go, emitting their fairy-light. I laugh and thank the little beings for showing up to celebrate my leaving Carlisle, as well as twinkling for my excitement at just learning I leave in two weeks to work at the Army's vacation resort in Garmisch-Partenkirchen, Germany.

CHAPTER 9

THE HILLS ARE ALIVE

2009

In Frankfurt, amid the crisp fall weather, I board the fast train to Munich, followed by a slow local train that wends its way south through Bavaria and up into the mountains, through fields dotted with dairy cattle and small villages. Alpine peaks tower against the intense blue sky.

Arriving in Garmisch-Partenkirchen, site of the 1936 Winter Olympics, I find the Hertz office where my black Mercedes compact is waiting, then proceed to an old German inn, Hotel Obermuehle ("family-run since 1634"), where I'll be housed for the next six weeks. I'm given a comfortable bedroom with sitting area, a tiny kitchen, and a large porch under the eaves overlooking a rushing mill stream, and I can barely contain my delight. The next morning I wake to the sound of cowbells. A small herd of cattle trundles through the narrow streets outside my window, on its way to a fresh pasture. Downstairs in the dining room a hearty buffet breakfast covers white linen tablecloths: freshly sliced bread for toasting, croissants, butter, cheeses, eggs, yogurt, muesli, fruit, and plenty of coffee. And there is a clean, quiet indoor pool as well as a sauna. Excited by this paradise, I sleep only four or five hours the first few nights.

When I report in at the base, the ACS director, a white woman in her 50s with hair dyed a pretty auburn exclaims, "Our new Merk! We're so glad to have you here. Let me show you your office." We leave the building and cross a shaded parking lot to another two-story red-roofed building and climb stairs to the second floor. Opening the door to a large office with desk, chairs, and two worn couches, she explains, "We want people to be able to see you in confidence without being seen by other staff."

I make an appointment to meet the garrison commander for this tiny base, curious to learn how I might be called upon. Only a few active-duty soldiers are assigned here — twenty MPs and just a handful of other enlisted, plus a few officers who teach at the Marshall European Center for Security Studies. The center is a German-American partnership doing research and offering courses to NATO allies on issues of transnational security. The other Americans are all civilians working in the Army service support structure (recreation, financial counseling, education) or staffing the nearby resort.

The commander's office is upstairs in a quiet brick building, probably the original headquarters of this German *kaserne*, or small military post. She's a stocky middle-aged white woman with short, straight salt-and-pepper hair who keeps me waiting only a minute or two when I arrive for our appointment. She's a civilian, but has the erect posture that leads me to ask whether she's ex-military.

"I was with the Air Force," she answers. "So was my husband. We retired and now we've both got Army civilian jobs. He works at the medical clinic in Ansbach."

"That's a bit of a drive from here, isn't it? How does that work?"

"This year we'll just see each other on weekends." She pauses, as if uncertain whether she wants to say more. Then she confides, "When you've been married as long as I have, that's actually a nice arrangement — I get to enjoy some alone time, and then we're really happy to see each other."

"So that's just for this year?"

"Every year or two it's something different. But we both love living in Europe, so we'll see if we can't keep finding jobs at the same base or close by, like this. It's great having you Merks come here, by the way."

"I'm delighted to be here."

"People think that because we're in beautiful Garmisch, we wouldn't have any problems. Couldn't be further from the truth. Actually, it's like living in a fishbowl — everybody seems to know your business."

"I know what you mean. That's why our rotations are so short. In and out, and all confidences go with us when we leave."

"And we appreciate it, since there are no English-speaking counselors within a hundred miles."

Then to my surprise, she launches into a revealing personal story regarding one of her adult children. We talk for over an hour. I mainly listen, and begin to have high hopes for this assignment.

ADJACENT TO THE GARRISON IS THE LUXURIOUS Edelweiss Resort — one of several destination resorts maintained for the use of U.S. military personnel and their families, with 17,000 guests each year. I sit in its spacious lobby several mornings a week, listening to the sweeping soundtrack from *Out of Africa* pouring down from overhead speakers. At first I imagine striking up conversations in order to build my activity report statistics. But as the guests come and go, absorbed with their families and their plans, I can't think of a way to approach them without intruding, and realize this would not be the time or place they would be open to talking about their problems. The working staff are too busy to be drawn into conversation, though I do manage to slip some of them my card. The large brown leather couches are soft and comfortable, and no one pays me any mind.

One morning, I hear a German-accented announcement: "The bus for Dachau leaves in 15 minutes." A prickling goes up my spine. My thoughts shift to 1940 and I feel alarm. People sit casually on the couches; some must be waiting for their trip to the concentration camp. Then a small group of warmly-dressed adults and teenagers boards the bus. Am I the only person here to find all this eerie?

Another day I'm sitting at a table outside in the sunlight, enjoying the resort's excellent coffee, when I spy a small group of soldiers talking and smoking on the patio about 100 feet away. The word "fuck" drifts to my ears about every three seconds. As these men in late adolescence showcase their worldly command of profanity, they seem oblivious to the awesome sight of the mountain, Zugspitze, looming over this Alpine paradise. Perhaps they're on R&R from a war zone and just haven't gotten their bearings. Maybe they just can't relax enough to see where they are.

Sometimes I treat myself to the extensive buffet lunch in the cafeteria of the Marshall Center, and of course I watch for unaccompanied personnel to talk to. One day I set my tray down across from a half-empty tray and go to get something to drink. When I return, the chair opposite holds a well-dressed man who appears Middle Eastern by his complexion and mustache. He responds to my attempts at small talk, which show he is an Iraqi government official, and we converse politely for a few minutes while I fancy myself something between a spy and a diplomat. The Iraqis are demanding that the U.S. forces leave their country. I frame a naive question about conflict between Sunni and Shia Muslims. His brow furrows as he assures me that his people are capable of solving their own problems. Given the fact that Bush's "Operation Iraqi Freedom" led to a full-on civil war, at the time in its seventh year and having caused the deaths of over 100,000 Iraqi civilians thus far, his comment shows remarkable restraint.

Twice a week, I take a half-hour scenic drive further up into the mountains north of Garmisch to a NATO training school in Oberammergau. The town is famous as the place where residents enact the Christian Passion Play once every ten years. Thousands come to see it. With the next production one year away, the small, isolated town is sleepy and largely deserted. Souvenir shops abound, but have few customers.

The NATO school sits on the site of a former secret Nazi military installation. U.S. forces initially occupied it in the postwar period, then turned it over to NATO for training in joint operations, intelligence, and security. The floor-to ceiling windows in the school's cafeteria provide a breathtaking view of the Alps. I lurk there over lunch, hoping to meet Americans in need of my services. The first day I see only one person in an American uniform; the others are dressed in an eye-catching variety of camouflage patterns, depending on whether they're from France, Latvia, Slovenia, or any of a dozen other countries. The patterns range from linear and pixel-y, to impressionist painting, to broad swaths of tan and brown. The Germans wear a particularly pretty pattern in shades of bright and dark green that makes them look rather like trees. But I find no one to talk to.

Another day I attend an afternoon "Hail and Farewell" ceremony for incoming and outgoing personnel. It's held in a tent-topped extension of the recreation center, where I mingle with Brits, Germans, Italians, French, Americans, and Eastern Europeans. By gruff tones in their voices and subtle twitching of their shoulders, I sense they may not get along too well. They seem testy and awkward with each other, though most are drinking beer. I sit down by a burly American sergeant and introduce myself. He smiles and points self-consciously to his tall liter glass of beer. "American soldiers don't normally drink during work hours. But see, it's a NATO thing. When in Rome, you know."

Only a couple dozen U.S. military personnel are assigned to this school. As one young specialist shows me how he operates the audio-visual system feeding into the classrooms, I explain my role and offer him my card. He firmly declines the card and says, "No, thank you ma'am. I'm good to go." His reaction is typical of the other soldiers as well.

The NATO wives, however, are a different story. I jump at an invitation to attend a presentation by the wife of the outgoing British commander for a group of fellow spouses. Later, Sue Jervis will publish a book, *Relocation, Gender and Emotion: A Psycho-Social Perspective on the Experiences of Military Wives.* As she prepares to leave her husband's posting this afternoon, she dares to share the findings of her dissertation concerning the effects on military wives of repeated relocation. It is a pointed feminist analysis of the expectation that wives will subordinate their aspirations to their husbands' careers, dutifully do volunteer work, and not complain about what they have given up.

"It feels as though it could be risky to your husband's career if you speak of your reservations about military life," she says. "You're supposed to be quietly getting on with it. And there's a loss of personal identity and individuality — you become an ID card, an appendage." Nods and affirming murmurs swirl around the room.

She speaks of her acute frustration spending five years in the extreme isolation of Oberammergau, and describes a syndrome of "post-relocation emotional disturbance" in which she and her peers have felt incompetent, disoriented and depressed in response to all the losses and dislocations. When she invites audience discussion, a Dutch woman stands up.

"This is exactly my experience, too. It's very painful. People don't realize how much we give up. Once I get back to Holland, I won't ever want to leave again."

Afterwards, a shy American woman with wavy black hair approaches me and asks for an appointment. We arrange to meet the following day at my office in Garmisch.

"I've just got to talk," she says, moving restlessly on the couch. "I've been in Oberammergau for eleven months. My husband is assigned to the NATO school for three years. I don't know if I can stand it that long. I'm so lonely."

She inhales sharply and looks across at me, then down at her hands clenched in her lap. I wait for her to say more.

"There's only one other American wife in Oberammergau and most of the time she's off traveling. The rest are from the other NATO countries. I had no idea what I was getting into."

"Are the NATO wives not friendly?"

"Not really. Oh, they speak English, they say hello. But none of them has invited me over or seems to want to get to know me. The Dutch women pretty much stick to themselves. There's a few others who seem to have a little clique, and they take trips together."

"And your husband — does he see what you're going through?"

"I don't think he gets it. He loves his job with NATO, and he's thrilled to be here in Europe. We get along fine when he's at home, and we've done some sightseeing when he's on leave, but the rest of the time I feel trapped. I've been an Army wife for ten years, and I never had to go through anything like this before."

"It doesn't look like there's much going on in the town, either."

"A few hotels, a couple restaurants. Hardly anything that's not related to that damn Passion Play."

"Not your sort of thing."

"Ugh." She looks at me. "I hope you're not Catholic?"

I shake my head.

"I just can't relate. I'm into history, but this is religious fanaticism. I don't think I can stand to be around next summer when the hordes descend."

I'd probably feel the same way. "It goes on for several months, doesn't it?"

"May through September. I've told my husband I might go back to Wisconsin and spend next summer at the lake with my parents."

"That sounds like a good idea. What does your husband think?"

"He says the weather in Europe is best for sightseeing in the summer, so I've got to make him understand how hard this is for me."

"And there's still this winter to get through."

"That's right. Last winter was hard. The snow is gorgeous, and I did take some ski lessons, but there's so little daylight! I got depressed and flew home for a while in January. I just wish I had even one friend here that I could talk to!"

I know there is a small American spouse group that gets together for a monthly lunch in Garmisch. I encourage her to attend in hopes she might meet peers there. I also suggest she talk to someone at ACS about volunteer opportunities. But her situation reveals a systemic problem with no easy solution. Dependents at remote locations do not have the robust support of Army services available at larger bases. They are on their own, and this normally functional woman is on the edge of despair from the stress of isolation. I'll only be here one more week, then I'm gone, too. Feeling helpless and sad that I can't offer more, I invite her to come in to see me one more time and promise to connect her with my replacement.

On the weekends, I hike the wide, well-maintained paths that rise from the valley floor into the local mountains. Germans seem to have an almost religious belief in the importance of walking in the out-of-doors, and have built numerous gentle paths, suitable for walkers of all ages. Elders with double walking poles hike these rocky hills and valleys of vibrant green. I can't help but sense these slopes are "alive with the sound of music." One afternoon, I walk directly from my hotel on a path that winds gently uphill, with benches at convenient intervals. On a knoll overlooking the town, I find a small chapel dedicated to the memory of local German soldiers who died in World War II. It is a sweet, quiet place, and the cream-colored exterior walls are covered with handmade wooden plaques honoring family members lost in the war. On each one is a photo of a young man, with a legend such as "Son" or "Brother." My eyes sting with the reminder that all soldiers are human beings with families, no matter who may send them into battle.

On one of my walks about the installation, I discover an adjacent woodsy campground with a small laundry house. Inside the rustic building stands a forty-something woman with blonde hair pulled away from her face in a scraggly ponytail, heaving a large basket of wet laundry onto the top of a washer.

"Good morning," I say. "I didn't realize this laundry was here. Are you camping?"

"That's right," she says, leaning over to toss the laundry into a dryer.

"All by yourself?"

"No, with my husband. He'll be back in a few days." She points to a campsite next to the wash house. "We rented that big old RV in Munich, but then he had to leave for a two-week job. Are you camping here too?"

"No, I'm working temporarily on the base as a counselor. Where did your husband go?"

"Iraq. He's a helicopter pilot. Used to be in the Army. Now he's a contractor."

"Interesting. What's he doing there?

"Flying combat missions!"

"Seriously? I didn't think contractors did that."

She straightens up and leans from side to side to stretch her back. "Neither did I. He got out of the Army after I got him to understand I couldn't deal with all the deployments and the danger he was in. So then he gets hired by a contractor and they've got him doing the same thing."

"But this time it's just for two weeks?"

"He's been there before and knows the drill. The contractors don't stay as long as regular troops."

"So what are your plans — if you don't mind my asking — for when he gets back?"

"We were going to spend a couple of months traveling around Europe — Germany, Austria. I've got some relatives in Holland

I want to see. But he can't be taking off like this. The pay is great, of course, but I want him to stop."

"Does he like the work, then?"

"That's the problem. I think he's still hooked on the adrenaline." She frowns and shakes her head. "We have to have a serious talk when he gets back. I want us to have time together and enjoy life."

I knew there were contractors like Blackwater employed to do security work in Iraq, but had no idea they might even be flying combat missions. I hand her my card. "I'm a contractor, too, but I'm a counselor. I'll be here for the next few weeks. I'd be glad to help you all talk this over, if you'd like."

She takes the card, but shakes her head. "He doesn't go for stuff like this. A manly man, you know. But when it's important, he does listen to me."

"Well, from what you said, this is important."

"You got that right," she laughs. "Thanks. I'll think about it."

In my last weeks, I'm on the phone several times to Malwell trying to get a follow-on assignment. I've previously refused Air Force assignments due to that branch's insistence that Merks report any airman who discloses homosexual activity. Many of my peers also have refused to cooperate with this patently unethical demand. But just this summer that requirement was finally removed. When the assigner learns I will now accept Air Force, she initially assigns me to Nellis AFB in Nevada, a site where personnel sit at a desk commanding drone strikes in Afghanistan, then go home for dinner with the family. I'm leery, but curious to get a closer look at that culture. But then the assignment is switched and instead I'm being sent to the Air Force Academy in Colorado Springs for six weeks starting in early November.

On my last weekend in Germany, I decide to explore the steep river gorges just outside Garmisch, which can be climbed alongside the fast-falling water, thanks to bold German engineering. Paths have been blasted out of the gorge's edge, and a cable handrail helps visitors scrabble up the slippery rocks beside the roar and tumble of rushing water. I make my way up and down both the Hollentalklamm and the Partnachklamm gorges, pausing again and again to listen to the voice of the water. It seems to be telling me something. "Strong. You are stronger than you know. See the energy in potential, then see it in motion — falling, dynamic, forceful. See that only in going over the waterfall do you achieve your true potential. Do not fear transformation. Life flows on."

This revelation shocks and exhilarates me. The colors of the fallen leaves — rust, brown, and blood-red — glow even brighter on the ground as I pick my way down the mountain, deeply grateful for my life and how this job has changed me. I've become more relaxed and confident, more skillful at engaging total strangers and more discerning about what each situation calls for. I trust myself. When I'm "in the flow" like this, everything seems to work out just fine.

CHAPTER 10

SQUARED AWAY AT AFA

2009

The intense sterility of the U.S. Air Force Academy in Colorado Springs is a shock. No Old World beauty and charm here. The architecture of the Academy is futuristic and cold in design — long, low buildings of steel and concrete with no soft edges or graceful shade trees. In this arid high desert landscape my eyes sting and my nose bleeds. I feel as though I'm in a spaceport, expecting something to land. The landscape feels gigantic, the scale inhuman.

The Academy is a 25-acre enclave within the 18,000-acre Tenth Air Base Wing, to which I am assigned for six weeks as the lone Merk. The airmen working here provide support services to the Academy, such as medical clinics, recreation facilities, and maintenance of infrastructure. It doesn't take long to notice that the Air Force culture is different from that of the Army. Air Force members are proud to be in the branch of the service that has high entrance standards, and even their camouflage outfits look sharper. When I report to work at the Airmen and Family Readiness

Center (AFRC), I learn I will have no office. But no worries, I'm told — calls for counseling are known to be rare. Air Force members have a reputation to uphold, not just for being smart and skilled, but also totally "squared away" in their personal lives.

But what about the cadets, the actual students at the Academy? A wire fence surrounds the main campus, and entry is strictly controlled. In my naivete, I did not expect Merks to be excluded. Now I see that the Academy Superintendent would not want an outsider like me to have contact with the cadets, who are being carefully shaped and indoctrinated into the ways of the Air Force. They're in a sort of pressure-cooker, and confidential conversation with an outsider might sabotage this situation. I do enter the grounds once, when a chaplain invites me to attend a meeting with him. But I am not introduced and remain silent, which reinforces my frustration that my presence is extraneous and unwanted.

A LITTLE RESEARCH REVEALS THAT THE ECONOMY OF Colorado Springs is driven by five military installations in the near vicinity: the Army's Fort Carson, Schriever AFB, Peterson AFB, Cheyenne Mountain AF Station, as well as the Tenth Air Base Wing surrounding and supporting the Air Force Academy. The Air Force units all have some role in what they call "delivering combat power from space," which includes operating drone aircraft in combat zones half a world away, and launching the ICBMs with nuclear warheads should that order, God forbid, ever come. Following World War II, the city fathers put a lot of effort into attracting the military to this high desert environment, and the result is this booming military town.

From the window of my hotel room I have a view of a modern five-story building covered in mirrored glass that reflects the colors of the sunset over the Front Range of the Rockies. Near its top is a discreet logo: Lockheed Martin. So it's not only the military here, but also its satellites — private contractors employing thousands of personnel. Hewlett-Packard, Boeing, Northrup Grumman, and Honeywell have offices. The building is gorgeous, a testament to the wealth garnered by the private sector in "delivering combat power from space."

Not only is Colorado Springs eighty percent Republican, it is also headquarters for so many conservative Christian organizations that it is known as the "Evangelical Vatican." It's home to the anti-gay Focus on the Family media organization, whose founder James Dobson wrote *Dare to Discipline*, notorious in the mental health community for its advocacy of corporal punishment. It's also where Ted Haggard founded his "New Life" multimedia extravaganza megachurch, the main hall of which seats 7,500. In 2006, Haggard was exposed buying crystal meth and soliciting a male prostitute. Reportedly that cut down on church attendance for a while, but in 2009 it seems to be very much back in business.

Saturday morning I wake up at 4 a.m. in the midst of a mini-meltdown. I focus on making myself breakfast. In meditation, I cry and wring my hands. Why am I feeling so anxious? Is it the aridity, the wide open spaces, or the barrenness of the dry landscape? Is it the conservative culture? Is it the Focus on the Family headquarters just around the corner from my hotel? I'm alarmed and confused and call Quin, a fellow Merk currently assigned to another Air Force base in Colorado Springs. We make a plan to visit the red rock formations at the Garden of the Gods National Natural Landmark.

On Sunday, we scuff along the red dirt paths, admiring the odd, beautiful rock formations jaggedly reaching for the azure blue sky. Quin's about my age, with short hair and a softly masculine appearance. Being an extrovert, her experience is different from mine, and she finds plenty of opportunities to talk with the airmen where she works.

"What do you talk to them about?" I ask, sincerely mystified.

"Oh, we'll talk about sports, then go from there."

Drat! I hate sports. "But what about with the women?"

"Lots of women are into sports. But maybe I'll ask them about music, or their hobbies, or their kids, whatever comes up."

"I guess I'm just not good at making small talk with complete strangers."

"You gotta be in this job. We talk about small stuff, and then maybe they'll open up a little when they know you better."

I feel discouraged. It takes a different kind of person to be forward like that. I would feel presumptuous, intrusive. Or, I wonder, could it be I'm just not that interested?

We shop at the extensive Garden of the Gods Trading Post, with many rooms full of local arts and crafts. I buy a painting of two blue-black ravens rising against a fiery orange backdrop. Later that day at the grocery store, I also buy an orchid, and then drape the furniture in my hotel room with colorful scarves. I take out the Gabriele Muenter art postcards I got in Germany and affix them to the refrigerator. I create several areas of focus around the room like small altars. This attempt to make my room a sanctuary seems to soothe me. Throughout the next week I read Buddhist books and listen to recorded talks. I try to be aware of the preciousness and fleetingness of this human life, to open my heart to receive others and their pain, and to set aside my own petty agendas. I ponder the Buddhist suggestion, "Regard everything as a dream."

But by the following week the effort to look on everything with eyes of kindness is wearing thin. I hear myself ranting in the car on my way to and from the base about mass culture, car culture, sprawling parking lots surrounding endless shopping centers. Why can't I find a single neighborhood restaurant or gathering place? I complain about the over-built streets with six to ten lanes and center lane obstructions to making turns. In this shrine of capitalism, you could spend your life shopping. Is there a connection between conservatism and a life centered on consumption, or is this just normal suburban culture? It gives me the willies. Nothing in this environment seems aesthetic or wholesome. Perhaps the older parts of town have more character and charm, but I never seem to locate them.

JUST A YEAR AGO, THE EVENING BEFORE FLYING HOME from Frankfurt following my first assignment, I took a bus into the central city with another Merk whom I met at the hotel. Carol and I strolled past the opera house and enjoyed a gourmet Chinese dinner in a restaurant sparkling with mirrors and glass. We drank wine, shared our excitement and hope for Barack Obama's election, and became fast friends. Her home is in Colorado Springs.

When I call her I learn that she is also working at the Academy, but in children's services, consulting with teachers and day care workers and mingling with the children. We meet to go for a walk together at lunch on a trail she knows inside the air base grounds. At first glimpse of her short, plump body and playful grin, a rush of gladness fills my heart.

She gives me a warm hug, and I relish the human touch. Soon she's regaling me with tales of her frenetic life. "My mother just moved in because she's getting a little frail and Tom and I just love it that we can bring her to live with us."

"You're close to your mother, then?"

"I think she's my favorite person. It's great to have her around. Of course, my daughter and her fiance have been living with us too, for the past few months. But now they've found a place for themselves and the baby on the way. So it's a regular circus at home. But it's fine, and we're all having a good time."

"You're going to be a grandmother!"

She laughs. "Yeah, ain't that something? So glad Mom will be around, too, for the big event. But how have you been? Keeping busy with the Merk work?"

"I'm doing fine. You know they actually sent me to Garmisch?"

"No! You lucky dog! I bet it was great."

"Fabulous. How about you — any foreign assignments?"

"No, that one in Germany was my last. I'm sticking close to home now and I'm so lucky to live here. There's always plenty of work with Fort Carson and all the airbases. I mainly do the children's assignments, because I love them."

"Sounds like they keep you pretty busy."

"Totally. Time flies and I like being there. Some of the children are pretty stressed and I try to get them to warm up to me so we can talk. And the teachers and the staff are such great people."

"Could I come and visit you at work sometime? You know, I haven't had any calls or any requests for presentations since I've been here."

"Yeah, it's much quieter with the adults. I'll arrange for you to come when we're having play time out in the yard."

"I get bored not knowing what to do with myself. How was it when you worked on the adult side?"

"Oh, you know me. I can gab with anyone all day long. I don't think I saw many clients either, but Frank the POC and I would chat and sometimes other people would come into the AFRC and we'd shoot the breeze." She looks at me with mischief in her eyes. "And I probably did some errands in town when things were slow."

We pause at the top of a rise in the trail and look off to the east where a wide, flat plain with sparse vegetation stretches for miles, perhaps all the way to Kansas. "Is it always this dry here?" I ask, realizing that my nose has started to bleed again. "I'm having a little trouble adjusting to the desert climate."

"Desert?" She is puzzled. "I think of this as the mountains," she says as she gestures behind us toward the stubby conifers that dot the foothills at the base of the eastern edge of the Rockies.

"I guess I should say, high desert. It's dry in southern Oregon, but not like this. But yes, the mountains are beautiful, especially at sunset."

"So where are you staying?"

"At the Residence Inn. It's nice, and close to the base." I want to go deeper. "I'm telling you, I don't know about this lifestyle. I don't mind being single when I'm at home where I have friends, but on the road like this it's hard. I try to connect with people during the day at work. But of course we're supposed to keep a certain distance with anyone who might be a potential client."

"Too true, and that would be everyone on base. The boundary thing. Well, listen. I'd love to have you over to dinner, and I will, but it's a little hectic right now at the house. Maybe in a week or two."

"Oh sure, I'd love that. Meanwhile, I'll just keep making the rounds, pretending to be friendly."

She bursts out laughing, "Oh Maureen, you're hilarious!"

She thinks I'm joking, so I smile along with her. But inwardly I feel that indeed, I might be a misanthrope masquerading as a helping professional. A far cry from the *bodhisattva* I've said I aspire to be.

THE AIR FORCE ACADEMY IS WHERE BRIGHT YOUNG people go to be trained for leadership roles in the Air Force, and where many astronauts have gotten their start. Rambling along a trail just outside the fence of the cadet area, I look down on a large open concrete quadrangle resembling a spaceport. Cadets in dress uniform enact a measured, purposeful ballet. They move in groups, all at the same pace, as if in a slow parade. Their dignity and smoothness remind me of monks gliding serenely along paths in a monastery.

One day, I am surprised by a cadet in uniform coming toward me on this external trail. "Good morning, ma'am," he says in a firm voice, with a nod and a smile, and continues on his way. I keep thinking about him and his fellows and feel more and more sorry for the pressure they are under to conform to minute details of dress and behavior while pursuing their rigorous college coursework. Even more troubling, I have just learned that many cadets feel pressure from their superiors to attend Christian prayer meetings.

That information comes from the Military Religious Freedom Foundation (MRFF). While researching the conservative flavor of Colorado Springs, I came upon an article about this organization, founded by Mikey Weinstein, an attorney and alumnus of the Air Force Academy. This scrappy advocate has filed many lawsuits against individuals and organizations within the U.S. military, fighting for the rights of non-evangelicals not to be proselytized while in uniform.

Earlier in the year, his organization collected confidential testimony from Academy cadets and faculty unaffiliated with any religion. Some non-believers stated that they attend Christian prayer groups and pretend to conform to this belief system because it is expected of them. Avoidance of prayer meetings would mark them as deviant, not on the inside track. Half of all cadets participated in a voluntary anonymous survey in which 41 percent of non-Christians said they experienced unwanted proselytizing at least once or twice in 2009.

Ostensibly against military regulations, evangelizing is what evangelicals do. This information aligns with my observation of military chaplains and other officers who regularly offer prayers in public settings "in the name of Jesus," and who seem to imagine that Jesus smiles upon their military service. It is chilling to learn that cadets in training, whose every action is scrutinized and evaluated, are subjected to pressure to espouse conservative Christian beliefs.

After two weeks, I have located no service members stationed at the Tenth Air Base Wing who have concerns they'd like to share with a visiting counselor. It seems everybody has been briefed repeatedly about the program, and they don't want to hear my spiel again. I'm restless and bored. I decide it's time to have a heart-to-heart with Frank, the Director of the Airman and Family Resources Center and my POC. He's an affable, broad-shouldered civilian with wavy gray hair and a hearty laugh, who fits my image of an Irish policeman.

When I stop at the door of his office he greets me in his booming voice, "Merk Maureen! Good morning! Come on in. Like some coffee?" He holds up his oversize mug and gestures toward the coffee maker in his office. I demur, knowing there will only be the Cremora I do not like.

"Anything happening here?"

"Here? What could happen here? Another day in Dullsville. No seriously, we're getting ready for an inspection. Some bigwigs coming in this week. Got to make sure all our files are in order, the pictures hanging straight on the walls, that sort of thing. I'm going to bring cookies."

"I like the part about the cookies. Should I come?"

"Sure! The more the merrier. Thursday afternoon. Stop by if you have time."

"Well, Frank, that's what I wanted to talk to you about. I have a lot of time on my hands. I'd be happy to meet with the airmen if one would call and make an appointment, but they haven't. It looks like you've done a great job of getting the word out. Everyone knows about Merks, but nobody's biting."

He leans forward and lowers his voice. "And that's the way it is a lot around here. We'll get a rush of requests for service, and then it gets quiet." He leans back. "But don't worry, relax! Enjoy yourself. Do you know the Myers-Briggs test?"

"I know a little bit. I took it once."

"Let me guess. Your high on the Introvert scale, right?"

"Bingo. And I'd guess you might be an extrovert?"

"Right you are. Of course there's a lot more to the test than that. I've kind of made a study of it. I'm in your field, you know. Got my Master's while I was in the Air Force. Always been a people person."

"Did you retire from the Air Force, then?"

"After twenty years, I was ready for a change. And my wife was sick of moving around so much, so we settled here. Plenty of work for ex-military in this town. And the weather's great. Did you know the sun shines 250 days a year?"

"I did not know that."

"And now I'm getting so old I'm planning to retire a second time! So anyway, the Myers-Briggs. I used to love to give it to people and then talk about what it shows about your personality, and how people can be so different."

He warms to his subject, and I try to pay close attention but it's a lot of work keeping up my end in this conversation that doesn't really interest me at the moment. Finally he says, "Here, I've got the test and some score sheets. You could take it yourself and score it." He gestures toward his bookshelves. "I've got all these books, too. Feel free to come in anytime, if you want to look into it further."

This sounds like an opportunity to escape, so I take the papers and make my exit.

NOT ONLY IS THERE NO WORK, THERE ISN'T EVEN ANYWHERE I can go and pretend to be busy. This enormous base has been designed so that there is no possibility of walking from housing areas to offices, or from offices to the PX and Commissary. No way for children to walk to the schools. Each area is separated from the other by vast empty spaces and it requires a motor vehicle to go from one to the other. I develop a pattern of stopping by the Family Readiness Center in the morning to check in with Frank, and then driving to another set of buildings to spend a couple of hours cloistered in the base library. If anyone wants me for anything, they have my well-publicized phone number. But no one ever calls. Maybe I'll get engrossed in a book about the gory military history of Alexander the Great, or one about the Taliban, then go back to the hotel for lunch. If the sun is shining, I might return to the base and make some desultory rounds, saying "Hi" at the Arts and Crafts hobby center, or boldly seek out one of the commanders of the various work groups to announce my presence so that I can mark this as a contact in my daily statistics. If the November weather is foul, I'll just stay at the hotel.

IMAGINE MY DELIGHT TO DISCOVER A BUDDHIST MEDITATION center in Colorado Springs! One Tuesday evening I go downtown to the Springs Mountain Sangha for their weekly sitting meditation. Their service follows the Zen tradition, but the calming effect is the same that I feel meditating with a Tibetan-based group at home. Afterwards, I introduce myself to the teacher, Sarah Bender, who is tall and willowy, and wears her short gray hair in a stylish cut. I explain my job assignment, and she tells me that she has been hired by the Air Force Academy to provide instruction and meditation at the small Buddhist chapel that has been created in the basement of the Cadet Chapel. She invites me to meet with her the next time she is at the Academy, and I am quietly ecstatic.

The day of our meeting comes, and I arrive early to explore the architectural phenomenon of the Cadet Chapel, just outside the cadets' fenced-off enclave. With seventeen steep spires of steel and glass, it looks like a set of rockets preparing for take-off. On the main floor of the chapel is a large Christian church with a vaulted ceiling. On the basement level, a carpeted room houses a circle of upholstered chairs with banners hanging above them, symbolizing alternate faiths such as Judaism, Islam, and Hinduism. To the side is a small room with a light hardwood floor, a dedicated Buddhist space decorated in spare Zen style. A polished wooden table holds a small Buddha statue, a vase of flowers, and a tray of sand for burning incense sticks.

Sarah arrives and offers me tea, and we sit on two of the black *zafu* cushions forming a circle in the smaller room. She explains that this space has only been here a year or two, and was established when a cadet pointed out the lack of space suitable for Buddhist meditation.

"I come here once a week to lead meditation and offer a short *dharma* talk. Not too many cadets come, but it's a start."

"What do the members of your *sangha* think about your working with the military?"

She smiles and blows on her tea to cool it. "Well, some wonder if it is appropriate, since we generally take a pacifist stance. But I've decided it's worth it to come here and share the Buddhist teachings with anyone who may be interested. And obviously, you're interested."

I find myself talking at some length about my own prior experiences with Buddhist meditation, and where they have taken me. In retreat settings, I've had insights that moved and changed me, yet I've long been inconsistent in my personal practice. She is an attentive listener, and I'm grateful for the opportunity to talk openly about the side of myself I rarely show in this military job. When it's time for the meditation service, we are joined by a man who is a member of the downtown *sangha*, here to support Sarah's ministry. On several occasions, I return to meditate with the group. Each time there is just one cadet in attendance.

SOON IT'S THE END OF NOVEMBER WITH A FOUR-DAY WEEKEND to contend with. I'm invited to Thanksgiving at Carol's house, where her husband is deep-frying a turkey. The company is amiable and the food is good, but for some reason I keep helping myself from the vodka bottle that sits out on the counter. I play ping-pong with her kids, then go back to the hotel and mope. I'm having one of those episodes when the desire for a heart-companion surges, and there's just nothing to be done. I distract myself for the rest of the long weekend with a trip up the cog railway with Quin to see the awesome views from the top of Pike's Peak on one day, and then a solitary drive to Denver the next. There I wander through an exhibit about Ghengis Khan at the Museum of Nature and Science, and then bundle up to go outside, where I trudge around a man-made lake in the dark, wintry afternoon. I am lonely.

On Sunday I decide to attend the Protestant service at the Cadet Chapel. Oy. What was I thinking? There is no comfort for me here, just a fundamentalist understanding of the Bible and video footage of the Three Kings visiting Jesus's cradle. The presiding chaplain packages his sermon as a Power Point production, complete with slides and bullet points. Neither the content nor his delivery uplift me. I practice breathing through boredom. In the evening my Merk friend Stephanie calls from a U.S. airbase in England, where she also struggles with pointlessness. "This is not a life," she says, and I agree. I feel so dishonest in this job, taking money for doing absolutely nothing. That very night, my Peace Corps frenzy begins.

I think, if what I want is meaningful service work, maybe I should join the Peace Corps. Many of my friends served and share the camaraderie of the returned-volunteer subculture. And no experience is required. From my online research, I learn that five percent of volunteers are older than fifty, and that few applicants are rejected outright. I call my friend Fran, who served in Honduras many years ago, and she encourages me to explore the possibilities. Her statement however, that she believes the experience did her more good than she did for the people of Honduras, gives me pause. Apparently the conundrum of struggling to be useful is often part of the Peace Corps life.

Should I brush up on my Spanish or my French? Could I get into good enough physical shape? Two years is a long time to commit, and at my age I might not be comfortable with the level of deprivation involved.

Moving on to look at other international aid organizations, it seems I don't have the skills they're looking for. I find online blogs showcasing Youth Enjoying Adventure and Randomness, with posts from people you might meet in a youth hostel. Maybe I really am too old for this. I learn that I could be paid to teach English in China for a year, and even go to the base library and check out an audio course in Mandarin. I begin to recognize there is a romantic fantasy operating, a hope that I might find a setting (overseas, of course — that's part of the romance) where somehow my gifts would be pulled from me and I would have the desired sense that, at last I'm being of some use.

It is helpful when a friend asks gently, "Do you think this is another way of escaping where you are right now?"

In the remaining weeks of the rotation, I drift through the weekdays and seek stimulation on the weekends. I visit the Cheyenne Mountain Zoo where I empathize with the orangutans lying listlessly in their cells. The gorillas look angry and turn their backs. The friendliness of the giraffes brings me to tears. I take a driving tour of the local mountains, passing through Woodland Park, Deckers, Pine Grove, Jefferson, Fairplay, and ending in Bayou Salado. There I buy a pair of earrings made by the owner of a small trading post, who also sells me a pound of frozen ground beef from her own pasture-raised cattle. She tells me that we're at eight thousand feet, so the wildflowers don't come out until June and the growing season is short.

This job seems to create in me a low level of torment, and I try to examine it for what it has to teach. I'm doing little good at all, so I'm pushed up against my own issues of purpose and "right livelihood." I muse on the privilege and comfort I have as a Merk — the nice hotel, car, and short stay, and contrast this with the circumstances of humanitarian aid workers. I've long admired such people and wondered how they find the courage to make those sacrifices. I figure they'd need to have some sort of solid spiritual grounding. I wonder if Buddhism might eventually help me find the emotional equanimity and the open-hearted ability to serve.

With two weeks left to go, I decide to spend the weekend at the Farish Recreation Area in the mountains a few miles from town, where there are cabins, camp sites, and a lodge for the use of active and retired military and DoD civilians. December is off-season — too cold to camp, and not enough snow yet to enjoy winter sports. Apart from one staff person, I have the place to myself. My small cozy room in the old lodge has a gas fire, and I can use the communal cooking facilities in a separate building. Now I'm really on a retreat. I sit quietly and ponder the thought-experiments I've been making about whether I could pursue some sort of foreign service. I recognize the dubiousness of this fantasy, thinking it unlikely I could tolerate the stress or feel genuinely useful. I realize I do not need to join the Peace Corps. I need to go forward into my life as a writer.

A writer? It's not a new idea to me, but an identity I've been bashful about claiming. I've grown restive with the clinical restraint required in psychological reports, and longed to write with greater freedom. Writing groups and writing classes have allowed me to play with a gift for words. And the enthusiastic responses to my email "reports from the field" make me consider that my encounter with the military could provide material for a book.

I quietly sing to myself, "Open my heart, let holy love flow through me." I go into a sort of reverie and write heartfelt prayers in my journal, asking to be relieved of selfishness and fear, to become more open-hearted, and to find "a human partner whose love and joy may enliven and encourage me." I pray to be free of hatred of political foes, to be free of smug cynicism and helpless despair. I can see that a sense of captivity is of my own making, and only open-eyed observation will enable me to free myself.

I write a letter to my email group, sharing that I've had no work to do and how I've been hiding out and biding my time, waiting for the six weeks to end. I tell them of my attempts to watch my own thought process and apply Buddhist understandings to my boredom and alienation. My kind friends offer encouraging responses, and I know once again how fortunate I am to have this community of supporters.

I'm still hoping for another assignment where my skills would be put to use, but my calls and emails to Malwell assigners have not resulted in any offers. The uncertainty about my future is worrisome. Finally, in late December 2009, I am free to stop the play-acting. I pack my bags to return home, with no inkling that within three days I will be hospitalized.

CHAPTER 11

COLLAPSE

2010

Soon after returning home, I am at the local hospital having emergency surgery to remove my appendix. Afterward, I see no stitches — my belly's wound is closed with some sort of stick-um. Then it starts to ooze because it's infected, so it's back to the ER to get it opened up, cleaned out. Ouch. Now it has to stay open while I visit the Wound Clinic several times each week. A brief pit stop for repairs turns into a protracted recuperation. I have to slow way down, and lie on my bed listening to music since I can't exercise with this sore belly. Even a short walk is tiring. My life feels random, dreamlike.

All through January I feel as though I am in a healing temple receiving treatments. Two healer friends guide me into a visualization, and in my belly I see a basin of yellow anger being drained. Then when a massage therapist does energy work, I tell my four-year-old self, "I will not abandon you." I rise from my bed to go to an improvisational dance class, and slowly dance "Recovery." At a workshop combining meditation and art, I make a "Soul Collage" in which a woman writer and an oversize tropical fish behold one another. I call it "A New Way of Looking at Myself."

In February, though I still feel weak, I agree to work as a Merk for a one-day National Guard event. After choosing a suitable uniform of professional clothes, I buff up my gold Merk badge and drive to the Armory in Medford. Family Day has been organized to support the families left behind when the 186th Infantry deployed last May. Long white tables encircle the large open space in the high-ceilinged, echoing hall. I set down a box of program brochures on the table marked "MRC," then arrange them in neat stacks along with business cards.

It's chilly, so I leave my coat on, surveying the room to see who else is here: representatives from local colleges, Tri-Care health insurance, Military One Source, Soldiers' Angels, and other military support groups. A woman sergeant bustling about welcomes me and indicates a side room available for confidential counseling, should anyone request it. In another small room, a teenage girl sits ready on a pile of pillows, with toys available for any children who might come.

I ask the sergeant if they're expecting many people, and learn they've sent notice of the event to all Family Readiness Groups, called FRGs. "Hopefully folks will turn out," she says. "You never know with these things."

Now there's nothing to do but wait. I sit at my table hoping to look available and helpful. After an hour, no families have showed up and I'm restless. I take a tour around the room, chatting with others at their tables. Some groups have free pens, keychains, and stress-relieving squeeze balls to give away. My employer has only provided hundreds of identical tri-fold color brochures offering a sketchy description of our program. I pocket one of the squeeze balls.

Across the room I spy a table marked "Chaplains," staffed by two cheerful white men in civilian clothes. Before I even arrive at their table, my inner Chaplain Rant has started up. I have a particular beef with the evangelicals, who now comprise the majority of Army chaplains, for not understanding "spiritual care" in a broad way, outside the confines of their specific beliefs. They see their religious duty as Christian evangelism, regardless of the lip service the Chaplain Corps pays to respecting other religions and serving soldiers without bias. The chaplains I have met so far have been open about their intention to evangelize and convert as many young soldiers as possible to their fundamentalist Christian beliefs. One described the military setting as a "fertile field for conversion."

But why do I care about this so passionately? I belong to a profession that emphasizes self-knowledge, individual differences, and free choice, and my job is to help people make choices that are right for *them*. If a soldier wants to talk over a personal problem, how can they trust someone who obviously has an agenda of their own? I object to the Army's paying a captain's salary to someone who uses the position to proselytize.

So when I arrive at the chaplains' table and see their stacks of camouflage-covered Bibles and Christian tracts ("Faith Under Fire," "Saved in a War Zone"), this subsurface anger is triggered anew. My Buddhist equanimity goes out the window and I'm unable to stop myself from asking, "But what if you're not Christian?"

The chaplains look surprised, and by the scowl on the face of the older of the two, I realize I have blundered. The older man walks away. Meanwhile, the round-faced younger man with rosy cheeks smiles and says, "Oh, we're happy to work with everyone in the Army. Jewish, spiritual, whatever. You don't have to be Christian."

Oh, sure. They'd be happy to convert anyone at all. "I just thought, someone might not realize that, passing by this table."

"Well, we are Christian, and that's why we have Bibles to hand out. But we serve everyone, that's our job."

He really doesn't get it. "That's good to know. Thanks."

I return to my table, the inner rant continuing full blast. For the rest of the afternoon, only a handful of people come in, and they tend to hang out at the squeeze ball table. At 2 p.m. all the representatives call it a day, and I too, gladly pack up my tri-folds and go home.

One cold windy night, I light a fire in my woodstove and take pieces of paper, writing on each one something I no longer want to influence me, whose power over me I need to neutralize: Provider Relations, Malwell Health Corporation, military entitlement, conservative Christian chaplains. I toss each one into the fire, saying "I commit you to the flames, may the energy be transformed." I need a ritual to save my soul.

The next month it strikes me that I'm sitting in a room full of books in my home, while reading the works of Thomas Merton, Matthew Fox, Mingyur Rinpoche, Eckhardt Tolle, Robert Thurman, Parker Palmer, Patanjali. This time off work for recuperation has led me to ask myself, "What do I really want my life to be about?" One day, walking through Lithia Park, I'm startled to hear myself say, "I want to give my life to God." What could that mean? Then I hear, "I am a writer," and that rings true. Asking that my creative side take the lead in my life would be a huge change in focus. My quest for right livelihood and a path of service has finally brought me to this point. This is my passion, my bliss. I dare to hope that writing my truth will be a service to others.

Soon it's spring and the flowering trees are blossoming, and when the lilacs and the dogwoods burst out, I become full of joy and almost giddy. I now see clearly that writing is my path.

In April, I take in eleven documentaries at the Ashland Independent Film Festival and learn more than I can really handle about video journalists risking death in Burma, and about corporations fishing Lake Victoria in Tanzania, sending the processed fish abroad while local people starve. And how in Nigeria filmmakers are arrested as they expose government corruption and human rights violations in the drilling for oil by American companies. The four-day experience leaves me shaken. The contrast with my privileged life is almost unbearable.

With still no indication from Malwell that I'll ever get another assignment, I sign up to be a 2010 Census worker, get fingerprinted and take three days of training. I go from door to door in the beautiful spring weather with others in my motley training group of semi-retired professionals, searching out people who have not sent in their forms by mail. This is Ashland and everyone is friendly. Some actually say, "Thank you for your service."

In May, I have my 60th birthday. My Mom comes up from L.A. on the train with her boyfriend Bob. Her old flame from high school found her and courted her after my father died. He's infirm in body, she's sketchy in mind, yet somehow they make the trip. We see a matinee of *She Loves Me* at the Shakespeare Festival and eat extraordinary breakfasts at their B&B. I get a lump in my throat putting them on the plane, hoping they'll make it home safely.

It's now been five months of no job offers and though I've

needed the rest, I'm afraid I'll soon be broke. I'd love to quit this dispiriting job, but have no Plan B. What's the holdup? Repeated calls to the Malwell assigners are not returned. At last, one says, "There's a problem with your status in the network." That's all she can tell me. My blood runs cold. I can't afford to lose this job. What does this mean? I finally locate a former supervisor who agrees to look into the problem.

"A National Guard chaplain made a complaint about you," she says. "You were supposed to have been taken off the list for Guard assignments, but it looks like you got taken off the panel entirely. I'll see what I can do."

That Christian chaplain who walked away!

The next week I get a call asking if I can be ready in two weeks to go to Korea for two months. Rumor has it that Korea assignments are difficult, though no one has given me any particulars. I feel I must accept. I go into a frenzy of preparations, frightened out of my wits, worried that in my weakened condition, I won't be up to the challenge. In my mind a soldier's voice says, "Suck it up and drive on."

CHAPTER 12

THE GIFT SHOP AT THE DMZ

2010

Carl meets my bus as it pulls into the station at Camp Casey, Korea. It's June 2010, and I'll be replacing him as the base Merk for the next two months. A tall and rangy middle-aged man, he has a cough and his color is not good. Once we get my luggage off the bus, he pauses to take a breath.

"Are you not feeling well?" I ask.

"It's this polluted air. Blows over from China. I have asthma, and I'm just getting over bronchitis. So glad you made it!"

His smile is warm and welcoming, yet the tension in his face shows how badly he wants to leave. He kindly spends the day demonstrating how to use the Korean subway and the on-base buses, and where to find the civilian staff I'll be working with, starting tomorrow. Then he's gone. I start to feel a tightness in my chest and scratchiness in my throat.

THE PREPARATION FOR THIS ASSIGNMENT WAS unlike anything I'd undergone before. A full day of online "theater-specific" training included videos on anti-terrorism policies and sexual trafficking awareness. I had to get a new set of fingerprints for an extensive government security check, and a special SOFA (status-of-forces agreement) visa. Then an orientation teleconference provided advice on Korean social customs including placement of chopsticks after using them. In addition to our passports, we were advised always to carry travel orders, SOFA identity card, and a certificate proving we'd completed anti-terrorism training. All that plus air reservations, done in less than two weeks. Then fog delayed the first leg of my flight to Seoul, and I missed the connection in San Francisco. The next flight was the following day and took fourteen hours, so I have arrived a day late for the scheduled in-country orientation. I'm jet-lagged and stressed, and confused about losing a day crossing the International Date Line.

The weather is hot, humid, and smoggy. A set of unattractive low buildings painted a lifeless putty color constitute this base, with a tangle of overhead power and phone wires. All colors are greyed-out in the polluted air. Just to breathe is unpleasant. The soldiers look awfully young. They strut about, talking on their cell phones, probably to girlfriends or family, seeming oblivious to the fact that Camp Casey is the American base closest to North Korea, ten miles from the DMZ (demilitarized zone). Beyond that two-mile-wide strip of land dividing North from South Korea rules a fiendishly cruel dictator. I'm not feeling at all blasé.

The next day, feeling strangely nervous, I make my first stop at ACS to meet the director, Mrs. Brooks. She's a middle-aged Black woman in a conservative, dark business dress, who welcomes me and shows me the small office I'll be able to use. My own office! She introduces me to her staff of three, who each have a desk and share the main room with the director. They look up briefly from their work, nod and smile. Mrs. Brooks does not have any special instructions for me, and seems eager to get back to whatever she was doing before I showed up. So I leave and drop in at the office of the base commander, a colonel, who politely shakes my hand but does not have time for a chat. I'm not getting any guidance on how to make myself useful here, and worry that this could be another assignment where I'm on my own to pass the time.

Next on my list is to check in with some of the many chaplains on this large base. Most seem to have just left after completing their posting, and replacements have not yet arrived. A free bus takes me to the far end of the base, known as Camp Hovey, where I locate a young white chaplain assigned to one of the brigades there, sitting quietly in his office. His uniform looks new and stiff as though it had not had its first washing. I wonder if he might be a newly-commissioned captain. He gives me a warm smile and says he's familiar with the Merk program. He nods vigorously when he learns I'm looking for space to see clients at this end of the base.

"Let me show you my extra office. Not too fancy, but no one is using it right now."

About twenty yards outside his building stands one of the only remaining Quonset huts on the base, a relic from the Korean War. He shows me into the spacious but dark room, lit by a couple of lamps, and gives me his extra key. I thank him and hurry away.

Back on the bus, I wonder why I scooted out of there so quickly. A congenial person seemed willing to talk, and with a little prompting, might have told me what he knows about this base. Maybe the nervous feeling I woke up with caused my shyness to get the better of me. Maybe I've forgotten how to act the extroverted Merk who knows how to keep conversations going.

The next day, I drop by the office of the Family Readiness Support Assistant who works for the garrison, coordinating the activities of the Family Readiness Groups for each company on base. These FRG groups provide family members with information about the soldiers' activities, especially when they're deployed. I bring in Merk cards and brochures and wait for her to get off the phone, noting her stylish glasses and dressy office attire. My khaki slacks and sensible shoes might not impress her. After a minute or two she finishes the call.

"You must be the new Merk. You can put those over there on the table. Are you embedded with one of the brigades?"

"No, I'm more or less 'at-large,' here for two months."

"You Merks don't stay long."

I'm not sure what to say. "I just got in Saturday — still a little jet-lagged."

"Welcome to Korea," she says in a sardonic tone.

Despite wanting to leave the building immediately, I press on, forcing a smile. "It looks like your job keeps you busy?"

"Better busy than bored. We've got a lot of FRG meetings this week and I've got to get the leaders the latest on the school."

"Oh! I didn't know there was a school."

"There isn't. But buildings are being remodeled to put one in, grades K through 6. They're telling people it will be done by September, and families with kids are already arriving. I'll believe it when I see it."

"Wow, that's only three months."

"Yup. Typical Army bullcrap."

"So you're an old hand."

"My husband's a warrant officer, fifteen years in. He'll quit at twenty."

"And you've been doing this FRSA thing for a while, too?"

"Yeah, and you know why? The families need help. The Army tells you what it wants you to believe. My job is to get underneath that official story and find out what spouses need and deserve to know."

She's tough, and I admire her savvy, but I'm unsure if she'll be my ally.

Later in the week, I discover Pearblossom Cottage, a large room in an old building's daylight basement, where three women lounge on comfortable overstuffed couches. Three small children play in the far end of the room, enclosed by a low plastic fence. A young woman with rosy cheeks and dark hair pulled back in a ponytail gets up to greet me.

"Come in! Have a seat. Are you the new Merk?"

"I'm Maureen," I say, reaching to shake her hand. "I hope I'm not interrupting anything?"

"Not at all. I'm Alice. I'm the director of Pearblossom. These ladies are Devora and Lisa, and they're pretty new here. We're just talking about what it's like to live on the economy in Dongducheon, the little city just outside the base."

"There's no base housing for families?"

"Not yet. This year the Army decided to go beyond sending just soldiers here for one-year assignments. Now they have the option to bring their families if they stay two or three years."

"We thought that sounded exciting," says Lisa. "But we didn't know what we were getting into." She looks over at Devorah and rolls her eyes. "We had to rent apartments in the town. The landlords hardly speak any English, and we're not quite sure what we agreed to in our lease, what the rules are. We're still living out of suitcases until our household goods arrive."

"And the school isn't built yet," says Devora. "My son is six and he's so ready to start school. They say at Camp Humphreys and Yongsan there is already base housing, and schools, and day care centers."

"Camp Casey is way out here in the sticks. They're not ready for us," says Lisa.

Alice explains, "Pearblossom Cottage is a first step until the day care center is up and running. Parents can come here with their children, but they can't leave them. There are all kinds of toys over there in the play area, and the adults can gather in here."

"Oh, this is a nice place," Devora says. "I'm starting to make some friends here. Our apartments are spread all over town so this is where we can hang out and meet other families."

"Maureen, please, come here whenever you like," says Alice. "You're always welcome."

This basement room feels like a safe haven, and I know I'll be back.

CAMP CASEY IS HOME TO TWO LARGE BRIGADES, the 1st Heavy Brigade Combat Team, and the 210 Fires (Artillery) Brigade, each with two thousand or more soldiers. The units each have an embedded Merk on a six-month assignment, which leaves me to handle other soldiers and civilians working in separate companies, such as finance, legal, postal, and military police. Of the two brigade Merks working here already, Fred is nowhere to be found. I locate Katie outside one of the freestanding cottages where the higher-status embedded Merks are housed. She's a slender blonde and seems startled by my approach. She gives me a limp handshake. "Pleased to meet you. Where are you staying?"

"Down at the Casey Lodge."

"Oh ... that's nice. Well, I hope you'll like it here."

"So have you been a Merk long? I hear you have to be in order to get one of these embedded jobs."

"Oh, yeah, for about seven years, on and off. But I've spent a lot of time in Asia. Maybe that's why Malwell sent me here." She's fiddling with her cell phone.

"Do you know where I could find Fred?"

"Who knows? And who cares? I never see him. And neither does his brigade commander. I don't think he does any work, and just spends all his time in his room."

As we are talking, a man in casual civilian clothes comes up, whom she introduces as her husband. Malwell expressly forbids us to bring spouses along to assignments. He sees my puzzled look, and explains, "I've got a military ID."

"Oh, then you're retired?"

"I used to work for the State Department. Right now I'm traveling, doing some writing."

"Are you working on a book?"

"We'll see how it goes."

"It's great you could both be in Korea at the same time," I say, trying to make eye contact with Katie as well, but she's looking down at her phone again. "Have you had a chance to do any sightseeing?"

"I'm sure we'll get to that," he says in a dismissive tone that I interpret to mean"What do you take me for, a tourist?"

My heart sinks. I've seen this pattern before. People who work for "the State Department," keep their distance, and are vague about their pasts. Typical CIA. I start to worry that I will have no peers to talk to. The ACS staff are polite, but don't seem available for camaraderie. Continuing my walkabout, I announce my arrival and availability to anyone who might refer people to me. Through the first week, my sense of isolation and anxiety increases.

I'm living "inside the wire," behind the guarded entrance to Camp Casey in a pleasant room with lightly-textured wallpaper that looks like pale green grass, and with a private bath and mini-kitchen. Since there is little work for me yet and it's so hot outdoors, I start to spend much of my time in this room, waiting for my phone to ring. It's cool and private and I can draw the blinds and sit in the semi-darkness, listening to the rhythmic "chunk-chonk" of cars going over a metal grate at the base entrance just outside my window. Beyond the base sprawls a dreary town where I cannot speak the language or even read the Korean alphabet on signs.

On Monday of the second week, waking up to realize I'm still here at Camp Casey, I groan and bury my head in the pillow, wishing myself back in dreamtime. I stagger to the bathroom, then pause to study the grumpy face in the mirror and tell that sad person, "God, I really hate it here." My prior admonishments-to-self to see adversity as opportunity have failed. The only co-worker I can find is frosty and not to be trusted, and Korea has a terrible climate. I can't get an intrusive image out of my head: I see myself blindfolded, kneeling with hands bound behind me, about to be shot in the back of the head. If that were actually true, it would explain my terror. I say to myself repeatedly, "Nothing bad will happen. You're okay, you're okay, don't worry." Sure, we are close to North Korea, but no one else here seems bothered by that. Am I picking up some hostile energy that others do not feel? Or feeling the unexpressed misery of all the people in this place? I have no one to talk to. I am definitely starting to panic.

In a program called Temple Stay, some Korean Buddhist monasteries offer the public a weekend with the resident monks and nuns. Hoping to find a peaceful antidote to my extreme distress at Camp Casey, I take the train south to Suyu station and find a taxi to take me to Hwagyesa Temple in the pouring rain. The lay temple ladies give each visitor a pair of loose pants and a vest to wear over our own shirts, so that we have a uniform appearance. We are served a tasty lunch of pickled vegetables, sweet sticky rice, glass noodles, mushrooms, soaked peanuts, seaweed, and soup.

In between rain showers, we're free to walk about the grounds. More than half the visitors appear to be Korean, the others American or European. I see no one with the ultra-short military haircut, though the monks and nuns have shaved heads. From a balcony overlooking the courtyard, I see the enormous, colorfully-painted Korean temple bell hanging in its own small pagoda. Vines with small white flowers drape down the stone walls of the enclosed courtyard. The sound of the rain is soothing, and I have a few moments of peace. I give thanks for the good food and the graceful setting. In the late afternoon, a resident American monk in light gray robes provides meditation instruction for English-speakers. He's a gentle and scholarly fellow who meets with a dozen or so visitors and explains the lineage of this temple and the forms of meditation and ritual used by the monks and nuns.

A light early dinner precedes more orientation to the temple's schedule, and instruction in bowing. The practice is to do 108 full prostrations: Stand, bring hands together. Kneel. Prostrate the entire body to the ground. Return to the kneel. Stand up. After just a few I am out of breath, exhausted, and embarrassed at my inability to continue. The evening program of chanting and bowing goes on for several hours. I feel hemmed in and borderline hysterical, and then at 9 p.m. all the women are led into a large room where we'll sleep on the floor on thin mattresses with woolen blankets. My jacket is my pillow. I enjoy the company of some giggly young Korean women who want to practice speaking English with me. It takes a long time to fall asleep.

We are awakened at 3 a.m. to begin the day with sitting meditation, bowing, chanting, and more sitting. After an hour I feel so sick from lack of sleep that I go to lie down and skip breakfast. But the mattresses have been put away, so I search out a quiet corner to simply lie on the floor. I now feel as trapped and alienated as I did at the Army base, but with a different cultural flavor. My only thought is, Let me out of here — I want to go home! Miserable and softly whimpering, I quickly pack up, call a taxi to take me to the station, and return to Camp Casey. I feel desperately lonely and friendless. How can I manage the two months before I can go home?

Back at the base, I buy meat and vegetables at the commissary and make stir-fry supper in the electric skillet in my room. I listen to recordings of the poet David Whyte that I've brought with me on my computer. He says it is the fate of the writer, the artist, to see and notice things on behalf of the group, and the task is to find the words that allow the expression. I write a poem about the kindness of Korean strangers helping me find my way. Something in me is being called forth in this extreme circumstance. I already sense that when I leave Korea I will not be the same person.

I use every self-soothing technique I can think of, but nothing really handles the anxiety. Meditation feels like more of a problem than a solution, since I usually end up rocking back and forth and weeping, not wanting to be here at Camp Casey. Nowhere feels safe; nowhere do I see beauty. My soul shrivels. I remain in the dark womb-room with myself, with the fragments of peace I can conjure. The thought that I might somehow be tuning in to the energy of North Korea is not a comforting one. I distract myself watching dozens of DVDs, escaping my surroundings. *Into the Wild* transports me for two hours and gives me a chance to have a long, deep, heartfelt cry.

I feel imprisoned, as though being punished. I feel old, weary, homesick, not up for this challenge. As though my ship is keeling over and I may drown. My life seems pointless. I know from experience that these thoughts are signs of depression. Madness looms. After a week of daily intense, irrational fear, I diagnose an anxious depression, and call my doctor in Oregon.

"I think I'm going to need to start the Celexa again," I tell her.

"No problem. We can do that."

"But listen, I'm in Korea on one of these military assignments," I say, trying not to break into tears. "I don't just need the prescription. I need someone to send me the actual medication. I can give you an Army Post Office address so it will get here quickly."

"All right. Talk to Susan, she'll take care of it."

Just hearing that this chemical boost is on the way is a huge relief. I need something to keep my mood from sinking to the point that I can't function. For the next week I cry in the mornings, wipe my eyes, and go out to act as if I am a real mental health counselor. When one day I actually meet with a client, it's good to focus on someone else's problems and get some perspective. Taylor is an earnest young white man recently promoted to sergeant. He's been brooding about his time in Iraq last year.

"We had to just sit there in the Forward Operating Base while the enemy lobbed rockets at us. We weren't allowed to engage them. I still have dreams that I'm captured and trying to escape."

I ask what his feelings are in those dreams.

"Frustrated. Angry. I want to get back there and actually fight those guys."

I wonder aloud if he wants to settle the score.

"That's right! Sometimes I sit around and remember being there, and then I imagine we just fire up the Strykers and take the fight to them." These are the armored fighting vehicles. "I can't stop thinking about it."

We talk at some length about his combat experience, and his feelings about his Army career in general. We also touch on his relationship with his girlfriend, who's ambivalent about marrying him because she says he's "obsessed" with his job.

"She doesn't understand how proud I am to be a soldier, to serve my country. It's my life's work. Nobody in her family is military, and she doesn't get it."

I respect his sense of devotion, but try to help him let go of feeling he is personally responsible to correct the mess our leaders have gotten us into. Of course I can't say it quite that way to him, but instead suggest he try to accept not being able to control the outcome, and to relax enough to enjoy his time away from the frontlines. He does seem relieved to have put all this into words, and makes another appointment.

Alice of Pearblossom Cottage asks me to give a presentation on "Stress Management for Parents." I prepare it and she puts the word out, but no one comes.

The weather is sweltering, so I'm spending a lot of time at the large swimming pool, studying the garish red and black tattoos that these young Americans have inked on their bodies. I find most of these images hideous. Sinking below the water, I try to mind my own business. Sometimes I attempt to start conversations, but it's awkward. I'm ignorant of popular culture and clueless on how to make small talk with people young enough to be my grandchildren. When people here introduce themselves, rather than ask, "How long have you been here?" or "How do you like it here?" they tend to use phrasing like, "How much longer do you have?" I'm not the only unhappy camper.

ONE AFTERNOON ON HER WAY OUT THE DOOR AT ACS, Mrs. Brooks says, "By the way, I forgot to tell you to see the NEO Warden about a gas mask."

"Gas mask?" This wasn't covered in my pre-assignment training.

"Yes, everyone is supposed to have one. Ask Mary about it. See you next week."

I turn to Mary, the soft-spoken relocation specialist. "Gas mask?"

"Hm. That's right... I think I was issued one when I first came to the base."

"What's it for?"

"Poison gas, I suppose."

"And what's an NEO Warden?"

"I forget what that stands for, but let me look up the number on our roster. Sgt. Molina, over in the headquarters building. Room 160."

Maybe Sgt. Molina can unpack this mystery for me. I take a walk to the headquarters building.

"I'm here to get a gas mask from Sgt. Molina."

"Sarn't Molina?" says the private at the reception desk. "He's gone. He PCSed last week."

This is a permanent change of station, base reassignment. "So who's the NEO Warden now?"

"Was that part of his job? I didn't know that. It ain't me, for sure."

"Well, what's NEO, anyway?"

"Something about evacuation, but I'm new here. Let me find someone who can tell you about it." He comes back with a staff sergeant, a stocky gray-haired white man with a Southern accent.

"Heard you're asking about NEO. So, twice a year there's a drill on evacuation procedures for everyone on the base. Civilians like you have to pack a bag with their important stuff and be ready to get on a plane or a helicopter, *tout suite.* The NEO Warden can give you all the particulars."

"OK. But who is that now that Sgt. Molina's gone?"

"Why, I don't really know. See, he wasn't a part of this unit, just used an office here. Let's see if we can't find a phone number." He turns to use the private's computer. "Ah, I see why you came here. It still says Sgt. Molina, but I bet he handed off the NEO phone when he left. If you call this number, that should get you in touch." He hands me the number.

As soon as I leave, I try it. "You have reached the office of the NEO Warden. Please leave your name and number."

The next day, a Sgt. Lawson calls me back, and I go straight to his office, which smells of stale reheated coffee. He has a friendly round face and smiles at me, so I get right to the point.

"I heard I'm supposed to get a gas mask from you. And what is NEO, anyway?"

"Have a seat. I'll give you this whole packet and you can read up on it. NEO means Noncombatant Evacuation Operations. We do a drill twice a year, in the spring and in the fall, so everyone is familiar with the procedures in case of a real emergency."

"Such as?"

"Well, obviously if we thought the North Koreans were going to invade."

"And what do you believe is the likelihood of that?"

"Somewhere around zero. But still, we're technically in a state of war with them and it pays to be prepared."

"So this booklet tells me what I need to know?"

"It will tell you what to pack, how much you can take with you, and where to assemble. Every year, we do actually evacuate a few people, just to make sure we've ironed out the issues that could come up. You could get a free trip to Japan!"

"And what about the gas mask?"

"You're a contractor, right?" He shakes his head. "We can only give them to civilian employees and dependents. Your company is supposed to give you one."

Well, dang. I'm at a dead end. If Malwell thought I should have a gas mask, they would have issued it before now, right? Still, I ask Katie if she ever got one.

"Are you kidding?" she snorts. "You know we can barely get Malwell to send us business cards. Fixing a broken phone can take months. A gas mask? Way beyond them. But don't worry, you probably won't need one."

ONE AFTERNOON, I TAKE A DESULTORY STROLL THROUGH the grimy, cluttered part of town nearest to the base in search of what I'm calling "monsoon shoes" to keep my feet from getting too soggy in the heavy rains due soon. I wind up with a pair of rubber pull-on Pumas. On my walk back to the base, I'm muttering: *Utter pointlessness, no exit, no liveliness or joy.* A tough week.

The next weekend, the best available entertainment seems to be a field trip to the DMZ — probably the only war zone on the planet that you can visit by tour bus. The fighting stopped in 1953 with a truce, but there was never a peace treaty, so the state of war technically still exists. A demarcation line was drawn roughly along the 38th parallel to form two separate countries.

Saturday morning it is overcast and cooler. We leave the base and travel south on the main highway, then north on a secondary road through woods, fields, and villages. The fog thickens as we approach the North-South border. The bus pulls off for a vista point, but the fog blocks the long view into North Korea. We continue on to the border, past security towers and fences topped with barbed-wire, to the Joint Security Area known as Panmungeom. Korean civilians are not allowed to enter the DMZ, so everyone here is either U.S. or Korean military, or tourists from other countries. We are required to sign a document saying we are aware our visit "entails entry into a hostile area and the possibility of injury or death as a direct result of enemy action," and it lists our rules of behavior for this entry. I sign it without fear since there has been no enemy action at this spot in over sixty years.

A three-story building sits on each side of the border, where soldiers of both armies stare at each other through field glasses. Directly on top of the "military demarcation line" of the border are three low blue buildings that are reserved for the rare meetings between North and South diplomats and Army personnel. A long conference table in each building runs north and south, and in the center the official border is marked. Our armed U.S. Army tour guide escorts us into one building for a look-see. Two South Korean soldiers are standing outside each building facing North Korea in a motionless *tae kwan do* stance. Their silent presence represents the strength and readiness of the Republic of Korea forces to respond to any actions by the North at a moment's notice.

The finale is a visit to the gift store, a small colorful shop jammed with cases full of souvenir items. Everyone from our tour bus crowds in. I wonder if I'd like to get a coffee mug or a baseball cap, or maybe a T-shirt with DMZ emblazoned on it. Or I could choose something more subtle like a spoon or a keyring with the inscription, *Panmungeom.* Or perhaps some generic Korean souvenir jewelry or a doll in traditional costume. I see commemorative plates, a letter-opener in the shape of a sword, flags, Korean soldier action figures, and scroll wall-hangings depicting ferocious tigers.

I'm dumbfounded by all this paraphernalia, this commerce in irrelevant trinkets that seems to mock the anguish of the location. The odd smell of garlic in the stuffy space and the press of bodies leaning over the glass cases makes me queasy and I hurry out into the cooler air. On the bricks outside, I recognize a slight, slender man with a pale, clean-shaven face and ruddy cheeks, and approach him. Earlier I'd heard him say he was a Merk working at Red Cloud, a base a few miles south of Camp Casey. His name is James. We look at each other in silence, then I say to him, "I've got to get a picture of this place." He stands beside me, and I hand my camera to another tourist, who snaps our photo in front of this remarkable, incongruous shop.

I've already taken a window seat near the front of the bus as James climbs aboard for the return trip. I smile and gesture to him, and he joins me.

"Do you think we'll make it out of here alive?" I say, touching my fingers to my lips and making an alarmed face.

"I don't know. Have you got your gas mask?"

"Ha! I tried to get one at Camp Casey but they wouldn't give them to contractors."

"Same thing at Red Cloud, but I'm planning not to need one."

"That was all very weird," I say, gesturing behind us as the bus pulls away.

"Korea is kind of a weird place."

"How long have you worked here?"

"Just since March, but I've been to four different Army locations now to touch base with the Medical Brigade. I'm their embedded Merk."

"Do you ever feel uneasy being this close to North Korea?"

"You know, I don't actually worry about it. Maybe subconsciously it makes some people a little tense."

"People at Camp Casey seem like they can't wait to get out of there."

"That's what I mean."

"Why do you say Korea's a weird place?"

He looks over at me. "It's just strange. Americans are sent here and perch in all these installations, doing maneuvers with the Koreans. Practicing for the war that never happens."

"Like time stood still."

"Exactly. Of course the Army uses Korea as a place to toughen up new soldiers. It's often their first duty station."

"So *that's* why they all look so young," I say. "Did you hear they're starting to bring family members here? "

"Oh, yes. Last year Camp Humphries was a constant construction site. Housing, schools, sports facilities. Now it's like a little American city."

"And who pays for this — taxpayers?"

"I'll bet they figure out a way to make the Koreans pay for it."

I look out the window, but there's nothing to see through the fog. The bus lurches along the winding road. I wonder if this man is anything like me, a reluctant participant in the military project.

I muse aloud, "That gift shop was surreal."

"That's a good word for it. Did you get a souvenir?"

"No. Did you?"

He shows me a keyring embossed with a metallic red "DMZ" and two lightning bolts. I raise my eyebrows. "It's for my sister. She has a sense of humor."

We ride in companionable silence for a while, then I ask, "Where did you work before you became a Merk?"

"I was a Catholic priest for fifteen years, and I had a counseling degree. When I left the priesthood, this seemed like a good way to get started as a civilian." An ex-priest. That fits. Another sensitive soul. Maybe he's gay, too. "What about you?" he asks.

"Oh, I got burned out on social service agencies and tried to do a private practice. But I couldn't make a living that way. I never imagined I'd end up working with the Army."

"And is that working for you?"

"Not really. I feel so out of place. Especially here in Korea, it's hard to get grounded."

"I can well imagine."

"So how do you feel working for the military?"

"It's different. But the Medical Brigade is cool. I've met lots of intelligent professionals."

"And then there's Malwell," I say, winding up. "They make me crazy. They're so stingy with information, have you noticed? So uninterested in helping with any problems we might have."

"Well," he says, "It is what it is."

I mull this simple phrase over in my mind. This is the first time I've heard it. It's like the advice to accept the things we cannot change. I suppose he's right. I do get wound up protesting things I have no control over.

The bus stops at Red Cloud and James stands up to leave. I already feel lonely again, as if I might start to cry. "I hope we'll see each other again," I say.

He smiles. "Yes, maybe we will," and then steps down from the bus.

I WAKE UP SUNDAY MORNING WITH THE THOUGHT, I want it to be a dark, dark day. Keeping the blinds drawn, I ponder that I have never before preferred such dimness to daylight, but right now it secures some privacy. I want to be in my own world, safe from others' expectations. The profound loneliness — maybe I am going to experience it fully this time. Not fight it or try to deny it. It's as though my heart is in hiding, out of reach. I write in my journal for eight pages, wrestling with my state of mind, getting in touch with old, core issues of self-doubt, of otherness, of not fitting in. I face the contradiction of being surrounded by weaponry and preparation for war while I am fundamentally opposed to that enterprise. This venting calms me and slows down my breathing. I recognize again how putting thoughts into words on a page helps me generate compassion for myself and acknowledge my own strengths. I feel an urge to post another message to my email group, and go right into describing my experiences thus far. Yet not wanting them to worry about me, I don't express the full extent of my desperation. I include three photos taken at the DMZ, and send it off to the people who have been tracking my travels and will want to know how I'm doing.

Before I arrived in Korea, the Buddhist teacher I met in Colorado Springs put me in touch with a Buddhist scholar named Wookee Jhin (who goes by Jean) living in Seoul. We connected by email, and she gave me her number to call once I arrived in Korea.

But I've been so nervous and overwhelmed that I haven't done so. Just after I send the post to my friends, I receive email from Jean.

There's a Buddhist teaching at 2 p.m. every Saturday at Buddhist English Library. It's located in Insadong, near Anguk Station, Line 3 Subway (Orange Line). The teacher is Ven. Cheong-go, an American who finished the PhD program in the Ohio State University and then joined the Jogye Order of Korean Buddhism. I can meet you at 1:30 on June 26 at the Anguk Station and go to the class with you, if you can come. We can talk more after the class. What do you think?

My heart starts to pound. My anxiety is still so high that I don't feel ready for this, but now she's asking me to call her. I'm so nervous and sweaty that I close my computer, leave my room and go for a swim. When I get back, there are already several responses from my email group, letting me know my writing has hit home and was appreciated by my friends. This gives me a warm feeling and I feel less alone. I'm able to call Jean and learn how to get to the subway stop where she'll meet me on Saturday. That night, as I turn out the light and go to sleep, I think, this has been, overall, a great day.

CHAPTER 13

SEOUL SEARCHING

2010

When a light breeze clears the air one day and the sky is clear blue, I hop on one of the Army buses that circle the installation and explore the other end of the base, known as Camp Hovey. There I come upon a small canteen called the Katusa Snack Bar that serves Korean food. Katusa is an acronym for "Korean Augmentation to the United States Army," and refers to the young Korean draftees who have done well in their English classes and are assigned to work on U.S. Army bases for the duration of their mandatory service, helping with translation and cultural interpretation. The snack bar serves beef *bulgogi* and other popular Korean dishes, so I sit down at one of the long tables and have some lunch. A brown-skinned American soldier, holding his tray, scans the room for a place to sit. He walks over to my table.

"Mind if I sit here?"

"No, go ahead," I say, smiling.

"I see you're a Merk" he says, glancing at my badge. "Cool."

"Do you know about our program?" I might have to give my spiel.

"Sure, sure. I've been in the Army a long time. It's a good program." He points to his food, "This *bulgogi* reminds me of a dish my mother used to make when I was growing up in Puerto Rico."

"Spicy like this?"

"*Picadillo.* Mm!"

"So what's your job here?"

"I'm a Master Sergeant. I help keep the troops in line."

"Are you good at it?"

"Oh, my God! Half my battalion must be fresh new specialists. They send them here for their training in ground warfare. And they're so *dumb*, so many of 'em."

"Why dumb?"

"These kids just don't know how to behave, and they get in *so* much trouble, especially hanging out in the Ville."

"What's that?"

"A sleazy couple of blocks right off the base. Full of juicy bars and juicy girls."

"Oh, I think I can guess."

"Yeah, it's nuts. The Korean government calls it a "special touristic area" and Koreans aren't allowed to go there. The bar owners all insist that these juicy girls they've brought in from the Philippines are just there to get the soldiers to buy fruit juice drinks."

"Doesn't the Army care about this?"

"All I can say is, they look the other way. They might send in the MPs if a soldier gets too drunk and rowdy. The thing is, everybody knows most of these girls are here because of sex trafficking."

"Wait a minute. Before I came here the DOD made us watch a video about sex trafficking that warned us to stay clear and report it."

"Sure, that's the official line. But the promoters have these women like slaves. They take their passports and then they're trapped."

"What about the Koreans — don't they look into it?"

"Nah. They pretend to object but don't do anything about it. Probably the business is good for the economy." From his sanguine tone, it's clear he lost his innocence about such hypocrisy a long time ago. "You should go there some time. It's perfectly safe. No one will bother you. Talk to the girls. See for yourself."

THAT AFTERNOON A PACKAGE ARRIVES FOR ME AT THE ARMY Post Office. I go directly to pick it up and return to my room to take the first antidepressant pill, knowing it won't take effect for a couple of weeks, but relieved I'll soon have help with my precarious state of mind. The rest of the week as I anticipate the trip to Seoul, I breathe shallowly, try not to inhale too much smog, and try not to feel anything. Another soldier makes an appointment to see me. Roger is an earnest twenty-something mechanic whose white arms are covered in dark tattoos all the way up onto his neck.

"I'm worried about me and my wife," he says. "It's hard being this far away. It's hard to communicate."

"Have you been married long?"

"Just two months. We met online."

"So you married just before you came to Korea?"

"Yeah, we really fell for each other. She's going to college in Georgia. She thought it'd be fine to be apart 'cause she has to study all the time."

"What happens when you talk on the phone?"

"She don't say much. I think she worries I don't love her. I just can't think what to say sometimes. I ain't got much education but I try. I'm in college, too, online. I want to learn to speak more educated."

"Do you worry too, that she doesn't love you?"

He looks stricken. "That's what I worry all the time. I think about my dad saying I was a no-count and I figure she might think the same way, especially since I'm not there."

"Whoa, I hope *you* don't think you're a no-count?"

He looks down. "Sometimes I do, yeah. I mean no, I know I'm not. I'm a Christian. I've got a kid who's seven now, with my first wife. I want him to be proud of his dad." His eyes brim with tears. "I just want to have a happy family."

Poor fellow. This has to be short-term therapy, so I don't ask him about his childhood or his mean father, but focus instead on getting him to name his good qualities, his skills, the reasons his wife might have fallen for him.

"I do *tae kwan do.* I got my black belt."

That's the ticket. I tell him that his homework is to write down critical thoughts about himself when they pop up, and to answer them with proud words about himself. We practice this a bit and then he's on his way. I assure myself that I'm not a freeloader on the taxpayers' dime, but rather someone who tries to do an honest day's work.

One afternoon, I leave the base on foot, cross the main road and go around the corner to The Ville. At the entrance to the two-block pedestrian street, a sign in English and Korean states that no Korean nationals are allowed. Bits of dirty paper blow about on the deserted cobblestone street. The doors of the low two-story buildings are shut, their windows darkened. The only sign of life is a little restaurant advertising its breakfast specialties.

The girls must be asleep. I learn nothing by coming here in the day, but keep avoiding a nighttime visit. This is not something I want to know about.

Walking this desolate street I'm reminded of a young soldier who told me that despite all the warnings of his superiors, he had married one of the juicy girls, largely out of compassion for her awful circumstances of sexual slavery. It was a noble act, perhaps a foolish one, as the couple's ability to communicate was limited. I feel powerless to change anything here. I stop and say a prayer of protection for these girls, and for the young couple.

SATURDAY FINALLY ARRIVES AND I'M UP EARLY, nervous about the trip to Seoul. It takes an act of will to push myself out the door. On the smooth, fast-moving train ride, most younger passengers stare into their cell phones. The women seem to prefer wearing high heels. Older Koreans look sturdy and stoic, and I see a few happy, well-behaved children. A man wheels a small suitcase onto the train, parks it, and walks up and down the aisle with a loud sales pitch for plastic raincoats, water bottles, and other items I cannot identify. An hour's ride takes us into Jongno station, where Jean has instructed me to change to the orange line and go one stop to Anguk, at the border of Seoul's old quarter of Insadong. The subway diagram is clear and the stops are named using Roman alphabet as well as Korean letters, so the travel turns out to be easier than I'd expected.

Still an hour early for my meeting with Jean, I look for somewhere to buy a quick lunch, but the overwhelming smell of garlic and the heat and humidity nauseates me as I exit the station. A bottle of orange juice from a tiny shop helps. Sitting on a bench, I manage to eat the hard-boiled egg in my purse, while watching the bustle of cars and people in this busy commercial district. The tall buildings, attractive large storefront windows, and artful signage contrast with the drabness of Dongducheon. A mist in the air is not quite rain, but I put up the hood of my jacket, returning to the subway entrance where we'd arranged to meet. A short Korean woman, neatly dressed in lightweight beige slacks and matching top, tentatively waves to me.

"You are Maureen?"

"You must be Jean." Uncertain of the cultural custom, I smile and nod, but do not extend my hand.

She nods, unsmiling. "Come. I am taking you to the Buddhist English Library. A monk is giving a talk." She presses quickly through the crowded sidewalk as I struggle to keep up. She seems rushed, remote, and I worry I'm imposing on her time.

We climb the steps to the second floor of an old building and enter a single large room with hardwood floor, tall windows on one side and bookshelves lining the other sides from floor to ceiling.

"You stay here," Jean commands. "I will come back in one hour and pick you up."

I take a seat at a long polished wooden table with a dozen other people, a mix of Korean and European faces. An American monk shares his excitement about a new English collection of teachings by Zen Master Daehaeng Kun Sunim, *No River to Cross.* He speaks of the master with reverence as the most influential nun to have emerged in Korean Buddhism. After years of solitary practice in the mountains, she founded several teaching centers to share insights to help ordinary people live peaceful, happy lives.

When the talk is over, I buy a copy of the book and peruse a rack of brochures about Buddhist temples and monasteries. These reveal the astonishing willingness of many men and women to walk the intense and strenuous path of monastic practice, which I tasted in my Temple Stay experience. By contrast, the Buddhism I've known in America seems lightweight — so tolerant, so forgiving. But I'm grateful to have had that opportunity to study Buddhist wisdom in a less arduous framework—and also pleased that Master Daehaeng is now bringing the teachings to a wider audience.

When Jean returns, we stroll through the streets of this ancient part of Seoul, a maze of shops, galleries, and tea houses crowded together in low-slung old buildings with traditional tile roofs. She escorts me to her favorite restaurant and orders the "set menu," a raft of small dishes is brought to our table to share. Mysterious new aromas emanate from the sizzling dishes, all delicious to taste. As the evening progresses and we drink the *makgeolli* (sweet creamy rice wine) she has also ordered, her face relaxes and she smiles more readily. Sensing more warmth from her, I relax, too. We discuss Master Daehaeng and her new book.

"A woman! Do you know how rare it is for a woman to rise this far in Buddhism? Or any field, I think. You know anything about Korean Buddhism?"

"I read one book by Seung Sahn Sunim, *Only Don't Know.*"

"Yes, he's very famous. He moved to America and teaches there." She fills my cup with more *makgeolli.* "Most people in Korea stopped being Buddhist and became Christian. Buddhism is something historical to them."

"What about for you?"

She hesitates, seeming to search for words. "I don't practice as a Buddhist. But as a historian I want to bring the rich Korean teachings to the rest of the world. It's kind of ironic."

"What do you mean?"

"Now that Buddhism has become popular in America and books are published in English, the Koreans are getting interested in it again. And they don't even know how much wisdom comes from their own Korean tradition. That's what I'm trying to share."

As we finish our meal and the wine is gone, she surprises me by saying, "You can write an article for the journal I edit. You come back next weekend. I will show you Buddhist temples."

It is dusk when we leave the restaurant. Strings of soft white lights hang from the eaves of the buildings, lighting the cobblestone streets. The temperature has cooled, and we amble over to the nearby Jogyesa Temple, home to one of the largest orders of monastic teachers in Korea. Evening services are under way, and we stand outside in the courtyard under thousands of colorful paper lanterns swinging just a few feet over our heads. Large windows on one side of the temple open onto the courtyard, and the enormous gilded Buddha statues seated inside emanate a powerful energy. We listen to the chanting of laypeople who alternately kneel and bow before these statues.

Jean leaves to go home and I remain to observe a ceremony just beginning, marking the 49th day after the death of a Korean nun by self-immolation. She took her life to protest a huge government development project (a so-called "restoration") of the country's four major rivers. A couple hundred people fill a small side shrine room, and I manage to find a seat near the back. Understanding not a word of Korean, I nevertheless resonate with the gentle energy and sincerity of their chanting, prayers, and spoken words. It all washes over me, and I feel a release of inner tension. A young man sings, backed up by prerecorded accompaniment and a slide show of the scenic rivers. Kind of a holy karaoke, very sweet and sacred. Feeling moved and mellow, I find my way back to the subway and return to Camp Casey.

The next morning, I'm still exhausted, but manage to crank out a second letter to my friends at home. Lacking a sense of purpose here due to the shortage of counseling requests, I console myself that at least I am a correspondent. After all, Jean has asked me to write an article for her English-language journal, *Buddhism and Culture*, and now it seems she's lining up events for me to write about. My homies respond, as always, with appreciation and encouragement, and I prepare to get through another week of this assignment.

I'M PLODDING SLOWLY UP THE HILL ON THE BRILLIANT white-hot sidewalk from my room at the Casey Lodge, headed toward another air-conditioned building where I'll try to appear as though I have something to do. I've taken to carrying a parasol, as some Korean women do, because wearing a hat in this humid heat makes my head even hotter. I've thought of inscribing the silk covering with "MRC" to publicize my work and my availability when I'm out and about, but decide against it. Too strange. Too arty. The idea makes me laugh out loud. Would anyone even know or care what those letters mean? I live in my own mental world ninety-nine percent of the time here, and often have odd thoughts like this and then question my sanity.

The week grinds past slowly and I continue to feel depressed and imprisoned. I meet with a soft-spoken young Army spouse whose husband is kicking her out of Korea — the Army calls it an EROD, Early Return of Dependents. She's resigned to his decision to place his affections elsewhere; she's signed a separation agreement and is seeking a divorce. From time to time, a bright smile flashes from her dark brown face — she hasn't lost her sense of humor. Together we contact Mrs. Kim, the Family Advocacy social worker. The plump, vigorous, middle-aged Korean woman bustles over to my office and advises the wife not to get an easy Korean no-fault divorce, as this will not protect her, but rather wait until she's back home in Virginia to file.

On Thursday, I join a group of Army spouses on a bus going into the nearby town of Uijongbu to tour St. Mary's Hospital, where the pregnant ones are likely to have their babies if they don't have enough time to get to the Army hospital in Seoul. Many of the women are dressed in flimsy, garishly-printed polyester dresses that hang unevenly on their overweight bodies. There's a clamoring in my head. Why are these wives dressed so badly? Must they talk so loud, oblivious to their surroundings and the Korean patients sitting quietly? Have they no sense of decorum? What must the Koreans think of us?

Saying nothing, I meekly follow our guide through the hospital tour. On this trip I am befriended by a middle-aged Korean woman who also came with us on the bus. She tells me to call her Riley. She's married to an American, and lived many years in the U.S. She now seeks out the company of Americans because, she says, she misses that life. It turns out she's a Jehovah's Witness. I'm amused to learn this, but don't mind a bit, grateful for her friendly overtures. I respect her church's earnestness in reaching out to strangers, and have found them unfailingly gracious when I turn them away from my door. She says she'd like to show me some sights in the Dongducheon vicinity, and agrees to call me soon to arrange it. A friend of any sort is a blessing to me at this point.

SATURDAY MORNING I'M OFF TO SEOUL AGAIN. A blind man walks unsteadily through the train, singing and holding out a small plastic basket for contributions. His humanity shines through his melodious voice, and I put in a thousand *won* (about one U.S. dollar). An ancient-looking woman appears, sits on her haunches in the middle of the car, and seems to hope we will buy her bruised and sad-looking apricots. Rising up from the cool underground station at Anguk, I'm hit with a blast of hot and humid air that causes me to gasp for breath and sweat profusely. I've never been so hot in all my life!

Jean picks me up in her air-conditioned car, her teenage son in the back seat listening to music with earbuds attached to his phone. He looks around seventeen and wears dark blue shorts and a lightweight blue rain jacket. His face shows little emotion, and he hardly speaks throughout our visit. She pulls over to the curb at a downtown corner and sends him into a take-out place to get us *kim bap*, a Korean version of vegetarian sushi, which we share as we travel to a modern temple on the outskirts of town.

The exterior of the temple's lower level is faced with red bricks, and a stone stairway leads to the second level where large windows on all sides illuminate the interior. Here, an artist has created on the interior walls hundreds of brightly-colored ceramic tiles depicting small Buddhas in a variety of skin-tones, each making a sign-language gesture. Read together, they are said to spell out sayings of the Buddha from the popular and accessible text, the *Dhammapada*.

The petite nun in charge has close-shaved gray hair and wears a soft gray robe. She graciously, mindfully serves us tea and asks me about myself and my presence in Korea. As we converse, I discover that being a native English-speaker means to be sought after as a teacher. She asks if I'd like to extend my stay in Korea a week after my assignment ends to help out with a children's summer camp at a remote Buddhist temple in the mountains. The program is headed by a British woman, now a Buddhist nun, who would welcome the assistance of another English-speaker. The camp is for children to improve their English as well as learn basic tenets of Buddhism. I am intrigued, and tell the nun I will think about it.

I consider her offer seriously. Would I be crazy to do this? Would I be crazy not to? Would I have to get up at 4 a.m. to meditate, chant and bow? And what about eating only vegetarian food, being drenched with sweat? But Korean kids age nine to fifteen — how precious. I'd learn so much about Korean culture and maybe some Korean language as well. But what if I hated it? Could I possibly keep on an even emotional keel? What if I just want to go home? Is that okay?

From the temple we drive to the 123-story Seoul Tower on Namsan Mountain, and ascend to the observation platform offering a panoramic view of all of Seoul. The vastness of the city is breathtaking — 25 million people in the larger metropolitan area, where 20 percent of the population of South Korea resides. Viewed from this perspective, it's clear how little of Seoul I've been able to experience in my short time here. We'd hoped to dine in the high rotating restaurant, but no tables are available until late evening, so we have a meal of barbecued ribs at the base of the tower and call it a day. Jean asks me to return the following Saturday, as she's got more to show me.

One afternoon, I run into Katie at the Commissary. She seems to recognize me and says she's invited the elusive Merk, Fred, to come over for drinks later today. Would I like to come? Daring to hope I might solidify some sort of human connection here on base, I agree.

Later, she and her husband sit outside their cottage at a rustic wooden picnic table where a large clear glass pitcher sits, beads of sweat on its icy exterior.

"Have a seat," Katie says. "Fred's on his way. Like some lemonade? You can add gin if you like." She points to a bottle of Tanqueray.

I help myself to a glass, adding a spash of gin to be sociable.

"So have you seen much of Korea yet?" asks Katie.

"I went to a temple stay at a Buddhist monastery, Hwagyesa."

"Never heard of it," her husband says. "You should get to Naksana out on the eastern coast. I sat with the monks at Naksana for about six months, once."

"Afraid that's unlikely," I confess. "I don't have a car."

"Oh, that's right," says Katie, pityingly. "You wouldn't." It doesn't take much further conversation to confirm that they lead lives much more interesting than mine. I finish my drink and leave. Fred never does show up.

Later that week, waiting in the lobby of the Casey Lodge for Riley to take me on an outing, the decision about working at the summer camp comes to me. I'm just not up for that extra week at the remote temple. One bridge too far, one toke over the line … or something, I mutter to myself. I'm not twenty-five anymore. Riley arrives in light summer slacks and a sleeveless blouse, accompanied by her young friend Grace, another Witness eager to practice her ministry and her English. Grace looks about twenty and wears capri-length jeans, a print blouse, and sturdy sandals. We drive a half-hour to Herb Island, a botanical garden with a pretty pond and a tea house. Grace asks permission to read to me from the Bible, and I sense she's pushing past her natural shyness to "share the Word" as the teachings of her church prescribe. I listen attentively though the verses do not interest me, so grateful for the company and the outing. We have lunch in the coolness of the tea house, and order *bi bim bap* — a classic Korean dish of rice with steamed vegetables and meat arranged on top, cooked in a stone pot and served with spicy sauce. I savor every bite. Then it's back to the base, my spirits sinking as we pass through the gate. But at least this difficult Korean assignment is now half over.

On Saturday it's raining steadily, and I spend time figuring out what shoes to wear to Seoul. My cute "monsoon shoes" are not comfortable unless I wear socks with them, and that defeats the purpose of being able to dry the feet quickly after being soaked. I end up opting for my flip-flop rubber sandals, and splash through the puddles to the train station.

Jean has said she wouldn't be available during the day, so instead, several of her women coworkers meet my train, smiling and happy to see me. In halting English, they convey that we will visit some temples and other cultural sites. We find our way on foot to the Bukchon Hanok Village, a section of Seoul where the 600-year-old houses from the Joseon dynasty have been preserved to exhibit historical Korean architecture. We wander through the winding narrow streets to the Bukchon Asian Cultural Art Museum, where we see artifacts such as antique musical instruments and costumes. The women put a wedding hat on my head, laugh with delight, and take pictures. We hike up and down hills (me slip-sliding in my flip-flops) to the lovely Gilsangsa temple. I sit for a short while and meditate, listening to the soft sound of the rain. Then we meet Jean at that same Insadong restaurant and have another amazing dinner, complete with many cups of *makgeolli* wine and much merriment. Fortunately I do not have to drive home, just happily find my way to the subway and back to the base.

EACH MORNING I WAKE UP IN DISAPPOINTMENT at having to leave the dreamtime, and count the number of mornings still to go. I try to redirect my thoughts from self-pity to considering the real opportunities of the present moment. Riley comes by for a visit one afternoon and patiently explains the pronunciation of the Korean alphabet, at my request. I pass the time engrossed in Gabriel Garcia Marquez's *Love in the Time of Cholera* and watch more DVDs from the base library. I cook more stir-fries in the electric skillet in my room. A store outside the base sells me a bottle labeled Makgeolli, but it is nothing like the brew in the Seoul restaurant and after two small glasses, I feel sick.

One day a soldier comes to see me and asks for assurance that our conversation will remain confidential. In a tremulous voice she explains she has missed her period and worries she could be pregnant. Her marriage is on the rocks due to her husband's infidelity, but they have still continued to have sex at times. She also recently slept with an ex-lover. And she admits she has still another new romantic interest, so if she is pregnant, the father might be any of these three men. Once she realizes I'm not going to judge her, she confides she definitely does not want to continue such a pregnancy, but has discovered some disturbing facts. Abortion is prohibited in any U.S. military facility, and abortion is illegal in Korea, though illegal abortion is known to be common. I'm horrified to learn that the U.S. government effectively blocks her access to abortion, legal in the U.S. since the 1973 Roe v. Wade decision. How could this be?

Research reveals that anti-abortion activism in the 1970s and 1980s opposed the use of government funds for abortion, leading to a permanent ban in 1988 on abortion in U.S. military medical facilities, with the sole exception of risk to the life of the mother.

While serving in the U.S., a woman still has the option to go off the base. But it is a quandary for women serving overseas in countries where abortion may not be legal or available. In 1993, President Clinton signed an executive order making it possible for a woman to pay privately to have the abortion performed at a military facility if she does not have other options. Anti-abortion forces rallied again to deny women this option, resulting in an act of Congress in 1995 that made even private-pay abortion forbidden in military facilities, with the only exceptions being rape or incest.

But my client doesn't know for sure if she's pregnant, so she's on her way to the base medical clinic, where they will at least provide a test. I contact Mrs. Kim again, the Family Advocacy social worker. It's true, she says, that a pregnant soldier would be in an awful bind in Korea. She suggests we contact medical personnel at the larger Yongsan base in Seoul, to see whether they have some idea about how best to proceed. If the soldier claimed she'd been raped, the Army would want to investigate the claim, so that wouldn't work. I wonder if she could somehow obtain an abortion pill, effective up to ten weeks gestation. Otherwise, unless her commanding officer gives her leave to return to the U.S. for an abortion, her only options would be to continue an unwanted pregnancy or to take a Chapter 8 "Voluntary Separation due to Pregnancy," and return to the States. Her military career would be over. She agrees to call me the next week.

ONE MORNING I WAKE UP WITHOUT THE USUAL teeth-grinding misery and compulsion to count the days until I can go home. Throughout the day I notice that the panic has abated, the nameless dread no longer my constant companion. Three weeks since starting the antidepressant, and it seems to be working. I still feel trapped and restless, but no longer desperate and overwhelmed. I attend a class in Korean *janggu* drumming offered on base and find myself smiling, finally relaxing into my surroundings without so much resistance. My mood is also boosted to have just secured my next assignment, three months at Fort Lewis, with six weeks to recover once I leave Korea.

Riley takes me to dinner at a large, crowded, brightly-lit upstairs barbecue restaurant. We heap our plates from a buffet of uncooked sliced meats, seafood, garlic, and vegetables, and sit on the floor at low tables where we cook the food on small burners, then eat it along with sweet rice drinks, pickled vegetables, and sesame noodles. Not once does she mention anything religious. It takes two hours to do all this cooking and eating, and I find myself smiling even more, having fun with delicious food and amiable company.

New Merks Martha and Rosemary arrive to replace the chilly ones I've gotten nowhere with. Both are open, curious and congenial. What a happy change! The older sister in me rises to the occasion and makes an effort to shepherd them around and share what I've learned. On Sunday, we take the train together into Seoul to see the Korean National Museum. The large airy building with much natural light perfectly illuminates the exhibitions. My favorite artifacts are the enormous Buddha sculptures and an exhibit of various styles of calligraphy. We have lunch in the museum cafe, then I leave them and go back to Insadong to meet Jean outside the Jogyesa Temple.

We sit outside on a stone bench, where Jean asks me to read aloud a speech she will be making, and she records my voice so she can use it to check her English pronunciation. I am happy to do this, glad that our connection can be useful to her as well as to me. And for the first time, she starts to talk about herself.

"My son is living with me now, you met him."

"He came with us to the temple. Did he not always live with you?"

"He was with his father, but his father is traveling a lot so I said I could take him. He's a good boy. A little ... young. A little different." I listen and empathize with her hesitancy to put words to her son's obvious extreme shyness and reluctance to communicate.

"Is it working for him to live with you?"

"It's fine, he can take care of himself when I'm at work. Being divorced in Korea, it's rare, and people shun you."

"That sounds painful."

"Yes. But I have my work, and my son, he's a good boy."

Just as I'm reflecting that having a son who is different might also be a cause for shaming, we are suddenly surrounded by a group of people involved in a Korean-American cultural exchange. We are invited to join them in a nearby building as they watch a video describing the making of one of Korea's national treasures in the thirteenth century CE — a complete set of woodblocks carved to print the *Tripitaka Koreana*, the basic texts of Buddhism in Korean. The milling of the wood and the carving of over 52 million characters employed thousands of monks, scholars, and craftsmen and took twelve years to complete. I regret that my conversation with Jean was abruptly interrupted, but we say good-bye and go our separate ways. Once back at Camp Casey, I collapse with fatigue.

I thought that might be the last time I'd see Jean, but the next morning an email announces she's bought tickets for us to see *Nanta!* next week, just before I leave Korea. The popular show involves chefs chopping vegetables and tossing knives. Her imperious command, "I will meet you at 4 at the exit 1 of Sinsa station," makes me smile. Well, okay, one last trip to Seoul coming up.

From then on, I hunker down for my last days on this assignment and wait to exhale. I'm thoroughly depleted, too tired even to go to the pool to swim. On Monday, I make a perfunctory appearance at ACS, where there's a request to give a presentation on resiliency to one of the military units later in the week. I agree, smiling at the irony of needing to appear an expert on that subject. Meanwhile, the heavily-tattooed Roger makes a second appointment.

When he arrives, he slumps into a chair and groans, "I'm so depressed. I blew it. I think my marriage might be over."

I ask what happened.

"I told her a lie and she found out. It wasn't a big deal. She'd asked me if I'd told my mother about her little brother being in prison, and I said no because she'd told me not to mention it, and then she finds out my mother *does* know and she's furious."

"Okay, she's mad, but why would your marriage be over?"

"She's so hurt, she's like a wounded animal. She says she can't trust me anymore. She even said I'm lucky she didn't file for divorce. She was abused in her past, and me lying just set her off."

"Did this just happen?"

"Last week. Wednesday maybe. And I've called her in Georgia every day since but she says not to call so much. But I can't help it, I really want to fix this!"

He's a mechanic. Of course he wants to fix it. He's so wound up that I invite him to do some gentle, quiet breathing exercises with me so we can look at the situation more calmly. As in our prior session, I try to help him move from self-condemnation to self-acceptance. This will be our last meeting, so I throw everything at him: serenity, relaxation, trust yourself, be impeccable with your word, exercise restraint. Pray for strength, patience, and self-knowledge. And maybe, consider taking leave to go see your wife. No doubt it's too much for him to take in, but it's what I've got and I hope it helps.

The possibly pregnant soldier calls to let me know it was a false alarm, thank God. Her voice filled with relief, she soberly states her intention to be more careful in the future. Then I spend the rest of the day in my hotel room reading. I feel what a sanctuary this room has been for me, and even start to think I'll miss it when I leave.

Despite my best efforts, I've been able to decipher very little of the complexities of Korean history, culture, and rapid social change. But I am deeply grateful to Jean and Riley, who have served as keys to what felt like the locked box of Korea, and whose friendship and kindness eased my frustration, fear, and dismay.

The exhaustion persists and I feel my age. But time is now less glacial, and I'm able to be more in the present moment, noticing growing affection for these tough Korean people. Then Randall arrives. He's old like me, grizzled and chunky, with an odd sense of humor. I greet him with joy because he is my replacement. Only a few days remain for me to endure this so-called job at Camp Casey. I take him and the other incoming Merks to the Korean buffet barbecue, but they seem to turn pale at the sight of the tiny octopuses, and we don't have nearly the fun I had with Riley. In the evenings I laugh out loud watching old episodes of *M*A*S*H.* Packing my bags to leave in two days, I congratulate myself on the completion of this ordeal, and the grace I've managed to muster in the transition with the help of the Buddhist teachings.

JEAN AND HER SON ARE WAITING FOR ME AT THE TOP of the exit stairs at Sinsa station in Seoul. She's in a jolly mood, smiling and even grabbing my arm affectionately, unlike her usual reserved manner. She escorts me down the street to the Gangnam Nanta Theater, one of three Seoul venues dedicated to this popular show which has run nightly since 1997. Once we're inside the lobby, she disappears for a minute, then returns with two cans of Makku beer and hands me one. Her son is quietly sipping a Pepsi. Jean's eyes are bright, her cheeks are flushed, and it occurs to me that her ebullient demeanor might be owing to her having had a drink even before we met. Whatever the reason, I'm glad to see her relaxed and enjoying our final night together.

The show's completely nonverbal broad pantomime can be universally understood from the antic action. Three chefs are given short notice to prepare ten wedding ceremony menus within one hour. Choreographed bedlam ensues, with knives and vegetables flying and percussive chopping and clanging of pans in rhythm with a jazzy score derived from Korean folk music. The high-energy show is loud, vivid, and loads of fun. Walking back to the subway stop, I promise to send Jean my impressions of Korea and Buddhism for her journal. She thanks me again for getting "American treats" for her son at the base commissary (peanut butter, macaroni and cheese, guacamole, Cheerios). We don't hug, as I would with American friends, but we send good wishes to each other with our eyes.

Back at the base, my palms sweat and my heart pounds, picturing how I will hand Randall the business phone and my base ID card tomorrow and walk out the gate for the last time, catch the bus to Incheon Airport, and fly home to Oregon. And in the morning that happens exactly as imagined, and I can once again breathe deeply. Going home at last.

CHAPTER 14

BATTLE BEANS TRILOGY

2010-2011

AUTUMN

The THWONK-THWONK-THWONK-THWONK-THWONK of spinning rotors on helicopters overhead drowns out other sounds on the streets near a large field at Fort Lewis. A few hundred feet up, choppers maneuver as soldiers train for combat. I flash on the sound that opens each episode of *M*A*S*H* as those wounded soldiers arrive at the show's mythical Korean War field hospital.

But no, I'm here in the beautiful rainy Northwest, walking about Fort Lewis and admiring the crimson and burnt-orange maple leaves gently floating to the ground against the backdrop of tall dark conifers encircling the open field. I rejoice in landing this plum assignment for a liberal intellectual, forty miles south of Seattle in the part of the country where I feel most at home. Several brigades of Infantry and Artillery are headquartered on this sprawling "Joint Base Lewis-McChord" (JBLM), which is also used for mobilization of Oregon and Washington National Guard troops departing for war zones.

Once again I am awed by the vastness of the military enterprise as I behold the many line items required to keep it running: armaments, vehicles, logistics, housing, training, food, security, health and educational benefits, family support, and recreation. And I'm amazed that a machine with so many moving parts can get anything done. The soldiers themselves often remark on the general inefficiency of the Army and their feeling that they are not being used effectively. I do wish they could find something constructive for this organization to do while they're waiting to blow people up.

Every day between rain showers I explore the base, seeking out casual contacts to beef up my daily encounter statistics. At a small playground, excited preschoolers swing and slide, and I take a seat next to the watching mothers, forcing myself to make small talk: "Which ones are yours? How old are they? How long have you been at Fort Lewis?" I'm surprised to find that most military spouses welcome such overtures, as they are often in the process of getting acquainted with a new posting.

When it's raining steadily I head for "Raindrops and Rainbows," an indoor haven for parents of small children who play at the various stations: artmaking, dress-up, puppetry, blocks, train sets and other toys. The staff and parents are usually involved interacting with the children, but I try to appear benign and make attempts to join in.

If I haven't brought lunch, I'll visit an eatery such as the former Officers' Club, where plush carpeting, white tablecloths, and large windows preserve its former elegance. The food is now served cafeteria-style and limited to hamburgers and a few hot dishes from the steam table. Though always looking for possibilities to chat with someone, I'm still too shy to make an approach in these circumstances. I typically take a swim on my long lunch break, and when done, return to the ACS office for afternoon clients.

A TALL, BEEFY STAFF SERGEANT IN A SNUG-FITTING battle uniform walks into the office, accompanied by his wife. She's blonde with a pale complexion, dressed in jeans and a sweatshirt. Her hair is in a ponytail and she wears no makeup.

"Go ahead," he says, as they each take a seat on the black vinyl and chrome office chairs.

She clears her throat, looks down at the carpet, then up at me. "I don't know. It seems hard to talk to him since he got back last month from Afghanistan. He barely pays attention to me. When he gets home from work he's on the phone to friends or playing video games."

"I'm not any different than I ever was."

"You're different. Your mind is somewhere else. Me and the kids missed you when you were away, and I still miss how we used to be."

"Maybe I'm still thinking about the deployment. It was intense." He gives her a hard look.

I say, "You're still in battle-mind,"

He turns to me. "Maybe. Maybe she expects too much. We're fine."

A pause while she decides what she wants to say next. "When I try to tell you about the college classes I'm taking, you don't listen. Don't you care that I'm trying to get more education, more skills?"

"Yeah, right. That's good. Keeps you out of trouble."

"What's that supposed to mean?"

He smirks. "Gives you something to think about besides other men."

"What are you talking about? That was years ago, and we were both unfaithful." She turns to me, "He even brought another woman to our bed."

"Well, we weren't married then."

"Oh, please!" She throws up her hands. "Why are we even talking about this?"

"I've told you not to do that."

"What?"

"Make those gestures. Talk loud. I hate fighting."

"You just don't want to listen to me. Why are you being like this? I'm trying to get us some help."

"What help? We're fine so long as you're good."

Tears form in her eyes. She says softly, "You don't respect me."

He says nothing, drumming his fingers on the arm of the chair.

I'm not sure where this is going. "Do you feel you respect your wife?"

"Sure I do. As long as she's a good wife." He folds his arms across his chest and tightens his jaw.

"Okay. But what is a good wife, then?"

"Does her job. Doesn't run around."

He says as little as possible for the rest of the session. It seems he's stepped back from the relationship, and perhaps some of that has to do with the numbing effects of a tough deployment, but he won't go into it, preferring to deflect attention to old problems in the marriage. When she calls me a few days later, she says they've been arguing and he broke her phone, so I urge her to call the Victim Advocate, an Army civilian who deals with domestic violence. She cancels her appointment with me and I don't hear from them again.

The plain truth is, I never studied marital counseling in graduate school, nor did I subsequently seek opportunities to learn it. On prior Merk assignments I've managed to direct such referrals to other counselors, but at Fort Lewis, the majority of requests are for couples work. I'm obliged to take my share of these cases, so I have skimmed through John Gottman's *The Seven Principles of Making Marriage Work*, popular in Army circles. Smiling knowingly, I invite couples to venture into their uncharted territory of pain, betrayal, love and loss. They often arrive in severe distress, questioning whether the marriage is still viable. Sometimes after a session, I believe the waters have been calmed and hope has been revived. Other times, the contradictions seem insurmountable. When one partner refuses to come in, I offer reflection to the person in my office about the choices before them. I'm surprised and honored when one Special Forces couple returns repeatedly over my three-month rotation and allows me to witness their troubled relationship at a depth that is profound for all of us. Despite my lack of formal training, intuition guided me to the places we needed to focus, and they felt we'd accomplished a lot.

As if marriage were not a difficult enough project in itself, military couples also contend with repeated absences of one partner that disrupt the continuity of family life. Lengthy deployments create huge gaps in which doubt, mistrust, misunderstanding and unfaithfulness can and do arise. Young, newly-married couples are especially prone to these problems, not knowing each other well when they marry and agreeing to this Army lifestyle. So my aim is to talk our way to more understanding, less animosity, and re-encountering the love that originally brought them together. These conversations often seem useful, but most couples only come for a few sessions and I never learn the outcome of their struggles. Still, I'm glad to have six or seven appointments a week, more than on any other rotation so far.

At the Battle Beans espresso shop in the ACS building, I find a mascot, a Beanie Baby-like stuffed toy that is like a plush Mr. Potato Head. He's a brown coffee bean with a green Army helmet, wielding a machine gun in one hand and a coffee cup in the other. Entranced with this icon, I buy the little guy and take him back to the hotel to contemplate. It seems to capture the paradox of looking into the innocent young faces of soldiers whom the Army tries to convert into killers. So which is it — are they sweet young people, or are they killers? Is it a soft squishy friendly coffee bean, or is it a weapon of war?

WASHINGTON STATE IS KNOWN TO BE ONE of the least religious parts of the United States, where according to a recent Gallup poll, 47 percent of adults say they are not religious and seldom or never attend services. There are chaplains here, but they keep a low profile. A sergeant tells me he went to see a chaplain about his grief over the recent death of his wife. "He started asking me about my religious faith," he says. "When I told him that wasn't a big part of my life, his eyes lit up." He felt the chaplain abandoned his need to be heard in favor of the challenge of saving another soul for Jesus. The sergeant decided not to return, and instead called the Merk. We meet several times as he grieves and plans how he will handle the upcoming holiday season without his wife.

During the weekly conference call, Merks continue to be treated disrespectfully by our supervisor, who calls on someone each week to recite their three-minute Merk introductory spiel. We are instructed to redirect requests for counseling to other base services when anyone sounds even remotely suicidal. Likewise, if we sense the possibility of a domestic violence situation, we are not to see the person even once, but point them to some other services on or off-base. So a person in crisis will be on the phone with us ready and willing to speak to a professional counselor — and rather than have them come in ASAP to talk about their concerns, we are to give them the run-around with another telephone number to call for someone who can "better assist them."

The Merks squirm hearing that we are to avoid dealing with people who are asking for help, deflecting them before they even come in. The Defense Department presumably contracts with Malwell for Merks as part of an overall program to address soldier suicide, and to redirect people in this way would be neither compassionate, professional, or ethical. I cannot possibly follow this advice, and by the looks on the faces of my peers, they can't either. My own policy is not to turn away someone who has asked for help, but rather wait to see them in person to decide if in fact they need a different or higher level of care.

My studio suite at the Candlewood Inn has a comfortable bed, a kitchenette, good internet connection, big-screen television and a view of tall trees from the second-story window. Yet as the days grow shorter with approaching winter, my thoughts are increasingly depressive as I ponder global warming, deforestation, famine, extinction of species, and my own death. Feeling anxious and glum, at Thanksgiving I decide to make a feast and borrow a convection oven at the front desk to bake chicken thighs, and serve them to myself with steamed asparagus, rice stuffing, and pumpkin custard ice cream for dessert. An excellent holiday meal, and a boost to my spirits!

This rotation wraps up just before Christmas and I drive home, knowing I'll be returning for another three-month gig at Fort Lewis at the end of January. In good spirits over the holidays, I throw an open house party and serve clam chowder on New Year's Eve. I'm so grateful for the friends who have asked for my email reports from each assignment. Their warm responses have felt like a lifeline, connecting me to a community of like-minded people who extend encouragement as I travel to serve among strangers.

Then I fly to Los Angeles to visit my mother at her fancy retirement home in conservative Palos Verdes. It's painful to witness the loss of freedom in old age common to the residents, despite the outwardly pleasant circumstances. Mom is lonely since my father died, and she's not good at making new friends. She chats every day, though, with her old high school flame Bob, whose health is getting poorer. We take a drive to Laguna Beach to visit him and have tacos at a surfer joint he likes. Then I return to Oregon and have just a couple of weeks before leaving again for Fort Lewis.

WINTER-SPRING

Malwell Health Corporation is now leasing "Executive Housing" in the little town of Dupont, across the highway from Fort Lewis. I'm assigned a modern two-bedroom condo, complete with laundry room and attached garage. It's sparsely furnished, but I decorate it with small folk art objects brought from home. The prior Merk tenant left me a large schefflera and I buy a cyclamen and a fern. Bewildered yet delighted by these luxurious accommodations, I stock the kitchen with all my favorite foods.

I've been assigned to a small surge team doing redeployment

interviews with soldiers recently returned from overseas. For two weeks we meet individually with dozens of soldiers who are ordered to spend a few minutes talking to a Merk. We must assess whether they have emotional struggles that might benefit from services available on the base and make referrals as needed. This was to have been the task at Fort Campbell, but the commander there did not cooperate, refusing to make those interviews mandatory.

The first thing I notice about this group of soldiers is that about half of them have non-European ethnic origins. I see soldiers who were born in China, Korea, Puerto Rico, Vietnam, Pakistan, and the Philippines. Some are African-American, Mexican-American, Cuban-American, Asian-American, and many of mixed race. There are people from French New Guinea, Jamaica, Guam and American Samoa. Most but not all of the foreign-born have become naturalized citizens. The variety is fascinating, and my eyes are further opened to the many sources of recruitment in today's Army.

As each soldier sits with me, I ask open-ended, hopefully non-threatening questions. Some are unwilling to say much, and it's all I can do to hold them in the office for five minutes. But most spend ten to fifteen minutes chatting with me, and some who do have things on their mind will stay for twenty or thirty minutes and leave with a referral. One of my longer sessions is with a medic who shared her devastation in attempting to save the life of a seven-year-old Afghan boy whose legs were blown off in an explosion. The child was the same age as her oldest daughter. She is requesting re-assignment to a non-medical job.

Another medic with twelve years in the Army describes being assigned to visit Afghan villages and offer services to women. She was uncomfortable with the attitudes of the Afghan National Army (ANA) soldiers and the local translators who accompanied her. "They act like every woman belongs to them, like they're property," she says. She's been seeing a counselor at Behavioral Health since her return, to deal with her anger and sleep problems, and says she plans to leave the Army at the end of this enlistment and get a civilian medical job.

Another soldier tells me, "I was really close when a roadside bomb exploded. One man died and there were lots of injuries. There was an arm in the road. Just an arm, so weird. Blood and guts everywhere. It smelled terrible. I can't get that scene out of my mind."

A common theme is the war-weariness of non-commissioned officers who've had several deployments and are deciding whether to continue their Army career long enough to be eligible for the generous retirement benefit they can claim after twenty years of service. The lines of worry deepen on a Black sergeant's face as he says, "I've got to do six more years, even if that means more deployments, because my family needs the money. Once I retire, I can get another job and still collect my pension, so we'll do all right. Now, I just have to keep going."

A lanky young white soldier comes in tense and smoldering with anger. "The whole reason I joined was so I could go to college on the GI Bill. Now I've got a brain injury from when I was on patrol and the vehicle in front of us was blown to smithereens. The shock wave knocked me out cold. Now I'm having trouble reading and concentrating. Nobody gets it that I'm not the same. I don't know if I can even do college now."

But other soldiers say in their interviews that Army life is working well for them. Several enlisted soldiers are on the "green to gold" track, one that lets them work on getting the college education they'll need to qualify for officer training. One lieutenant who is former enlisted is now hoping the Army will send him to medical school. A Christian from American Samoa is both radiant and religious, spending his few minutes with me testifying about how blessed he feels. An enlisted woman says her grandfather fought in Vietnam and her father was in the Gulf War. She's proud to be carrying on the tradition as an Army nurse and calls me "ma'am" at least once in every sentence.

A pretty young specialist says she and her friends had their eyes opened to the lives people endure in poverty-stricken areas. "Whenever people complained about conditions on the base, we'd laugh and say, 'That's such a first-world problem,' because outside the forward operating base it was so much worse."

If the moment seems right, I'll often ask, "Why did you join the Army?" Some responses reflect a proud military identity.

"I always wanted to be a soldier, since I was a kid."

"I always wanted to drive tanks and Humvees."

"I'm from a military family. My dad, my uncle, and my grandpa all served."

"I joined after 9/11 when our country was attacked. I wanted to join the fight."

Yet many state their desire to improve their own lives.

"I wasn't getting anywhere flipping burgers. Couldn't find a good job."

"The benefits. My wife is pregnant and we need health insurance."

"I've got three kids to support. That sign-on bonus helped us get out of debt."

I learn more about the military experience during these weeks of interviews than I did in all my prior assignments. The sheer volume of contacts gives me a broader and deeper understanding of the impact of military enlistment on people's lives. I feel grateful that these young people have made the decision to answer the call to serve, even though I take issue with the battles they are asked to fight.

A talkative soldier from southern California who is due to leave the Army soon shares some complex impressions about the Army. "I made some really good friends and Germany was terrific. Good beer, good company, beautiful scenery. But this deployment thing — we don't know why we're there, really, and the people don't seem to want us there and keep blowing us up, so what's the deal?" He laughs, stands up, puts on his cap, and asks for a hug on his way out the door.

THE DAYS KEEP GETTING COLDER, and when it rains steadily for several days on end I get cranky. The weather forecasters in the Seattle area don't speak in the terms I'm accustomed to, such as "cloudy with occasional showers." Instead, they say, "Rain, with some sunbreaks in the afternoon." These sunbreaks, they're a real and precious thing, and I'm inclined to run outside and turn my face to the sun when I notice a break is happening. Having little occasion to be otherwise outdoors during this dank and dreary time, I spend a lot of time watching cable news covering the so-called Arab Spring. It's thrilling to see people rise up against tyrannical rulers in Tunisia, Libya, Egypt, and other states in North Africa and the Middle East. I allow myself to hope that real and positive change is afoot.

In other news from Afghanistan, a Taliban fighter lays his weapon on the ground, grinning. A seeming surrender could only be a strategy. Military leadership keeps insisting it is only a matter of time before the Taliban "sue for peace," desperate to end the war against the mighty U.S. But the Taliban have the advantage of living locally, motivated by nationalistic and religious zeal, and surrender seems unlikely to me. Then there are the bored, skeptical faces of the bearded Afghan elders patiently listening to the young Army captain's explanation of the U.S. intention to help their country. I think we're in over our heads.

That's too disheartening to think about. So then I pick up Valerie Plame's fascinating book, *Fair Game*, in which she describes her life with the CIA and the end of her career when the G.W. Bush White House "outed" her as a spy in retaliation for her husband's criticism of that administration. This leads me to Tim Weiner's grim history of the CIA, *Legacy of Ashes*, which documents sixty years of the U.S. installing and supporting dictatorships in the name of "anticommunism." These books do nothing to improve my mood. But I confess, that's how I'm spending much of my leisure time this winter, suffering in the dark.

Specialist Shamaya comes in with her husband Lewis, a four-year-old they call Junior, and an eight-month-old infant. Lewis is wearing baggy scarlet red chino pants riding halfway down his butt, barely held in place by a cloth belt. He shambles into the room, slouches into a chair with his legs outstretched. He's scowling and minimally communicative. He pays no attention to the children except when they annoy him.

"We've been together four years," she begins, "me and Lewis and his son Junior, who was just a baby when we met. But ever since our son Jordan was born last October and we left Fort Hood, Lewis hardly talks to me. His brother was living with us here but he was so disrespectful to me that I kicked him out."

"And there went our free child care," he snarls.

"So you didn't even care how he talked to me? Called me a bitch and worse?"

"So what? Means he's got a pair. It's your own fault for nagging at him. He just had to man up, not take shit from a female."

I'm floored by his attitude, but Shamaya barely reacts. At a loss, I ask them, "What are you doing about child care now?" He glares at me, eyes narrowed.

"Well, now Lewis watches them," she says. "He was working but he quit."

"They took almost my whole paycheck for child support. I couldn't have that."

Apparently, he has other children living elsewhere. When Junior was four months old, Lewis got together with Shamaya. He doesn't want to talk about the problems with the baby-momma that led to his having custody of Junior.

On one thing they agree: lack of money in the household prevents them from going out and doing things they enjoy. They're not interested in my suggestion that there might be fun things to do that don't cost money. Having material things is the point. Her complaints about him fall on deaf ears. "A man should have the final say," he says. He remains testy throughout the rest of the session and little light is shed on what is eating him.

Shamaya comes in on her own the next week, and pours out the story of drug use and poverty in her family, and the imprisonment of her father. "After where I came from, Lewis looked pretty good," she says with a wry smile. She assures me that despite her toleration of his male chauvinism, she sees herself as a strong-minded and independent woman. When I express concern about how this relationship may be affecting her self-esteem, she straightens up and says, "I'm pulling back from my family, and I'm going to do more for myself. Go to Zumba. Get off the base on the weekends."

I never see Lewis again, but Shamaya comes in four more times, saying it's good to have someone to talk to. She doesn't have friends, she says, because they've betrayed or abandoned her in the past. "I'm lonely. Jordan is the only person I'm sure loves me." She continues to enumerate the ways Lewis lets her down: getting a DUI and not dealing with ensuing legal requirements, failing to straighten out his child support issues, not making calls he promised to make about their household bills, not looking for work. At one point she says if he doesn't do some of these things promptly, she'll take the baby and go to her aunt's, but she does not act on this threat. His constant irritable mood gets her down, and he avoids talking to her, preferring to play computer games.

Her Army career is also not going well. Her free spirit has not adapted to the seeming arbitrariness of the orders she's given, and she feels her female platoon leader has it in for her. I've now been working with the Army long enough to know that her negative reactions to the Army's way of doing business will impede her being promoted, but how to say this gently? It may be hard for her to endure the four years remaining on her six-year enlistment. After she cancels an appointment, I do not hear from her again before my assignment ends. But I continue to think about her in my off-hours — remembering Lewis's red pants and bad attitude, admiring her courage in joining the Army to escape from her unhappy family, and wishing I could have done more to help.

ONE AFTERNOON, WANDERING ON THE BASE, I come upon a celebration sponsored by BOSS, Better Opportunities for Single Soldiers. A live band plays rock tunes and the air is filled with the smell of grilling hot dogs. At one of the information booths, gals in eye-catching outfits of fishnet hose and leotards talk excitedly about roller derby, which is apparently experiencing a revival on military installations. Female soldiers and family members over eighteen are invited to join, and this weekend the two new start-up teams on this base, the GI Janes and the Bombshell Betties, are going head to head at the skating rink. The Bettie Brigade, they call their operation.

I can't resist. On Saturday night I drive back to the base, buy a plate of Filipino food outside the skating rink, and go in. Families and children occupy the bleachers — there's excellent ringside seating for the bout. A half-dozen people sip Bud Light at a small roped-off beer garden. A girl of around ten skates back and forth with a sign that urges "Go Betties!" The program lists the players, who've taken intimidating handles like Anna Mosity, Candied Slams, and Ivanna RuleU. Some are wearing those torn fishnet hose, others have dark tights or leggings. The Betties have baby blue tank tops, and the Janes wear tops of Army olive green. All wear helmets, knee, elbow and wrist guards, with player numbers written in marking pen on their upper arms. The match is exciting, with many trips and tumbles, but no one is hurt. Due to the swift and agile skating of their star "jammer," the GI Janes just can't be beat, and they chalk up their third victory against the Betties. Everyone looks relaxed and happy at this event. You almost wouldn't know there was a war on.

Back in the office, we are now instructed to hand out a satisfaction survey form to our clients, with a return envelope addressed to Virginia Tech University where results will be tallied. Our supervisor hints that these should not go to clients we imagine might complain. It's obvious we could simply fill them out ourselves and send them in. Perhaps some Merks did just that. Not wanting to participate in this bogus survey, I hand out none. And I am not surprised later to learn that the Merk program gets a 98 percent satisfaction rating that Malwell can brag about to the Department of Defense.

This survey is doubtless a response to greater scrutiny of the Merk program by the DOD, which has begun to demand more accountability and economy. Thus, I may be one of the last non-locals assigned to this base, as preference is now given to counselors who do not require housing or long-distance transportation. This creates greater tension among the Merks, who are now competing with each other on the basis of how little compensation they are willing to accept. Some are now securing and sharing apartments in the area in order to remain available to work at Fort Lewis. Others survive by living in their RVs.

I consider relocating to Olympia, a liberal town with three colleges and two food co-ops where I've been spending time on the weekends. The self-conscious radicalism there reminds me of the countercultural 1970s, with some young people dressed like old-fashioned hippies in long skirts, tie-dye, and dreadlocks. Yoga classes and musical events abound there, and I can hang out at a real brick-and-mortar bookstore. A few women connect with me through Match.com and we go out. Although nothing develops from that, it seems Olympia may have greater potential to meet a new partner than southern Oregon.

In the five-week break that follows this assignment, I manage to replace my broken refrigerator, buy a new phone, and visit my mother in southern California again, as well as my relatives in the Bay Area. A long weekend date with a woman in Santa Cruz is a disappointment because alas, "She's just not that into me." In Ashland I take Buddhist classes, dance classes, and swim at the hot springs. The downtown art house theater screens *The Welcome*, a documentary of the veterans' poetry retreat and performance in Ashland that I attended three years ago just before starting the Merk job. Then I'm back on the road, heading north.

SUMMER

Because of the new austerity program, no longer will housing or transportation be provided to Merks working at Fort Lewis. There are no military bases within commuting range of my home, so despite what it will mean to my net income, I start looking for a place to live for the summer. Luckily, I discover a small furnished rental on a tiny lake in a residential part of Lacey, just south of Fort Lewis, available for the whole summer. Gleeful at my good fortune, I bring my kayak, and circumnavigate the lake on several occasions. In June, Olympia holds its whimsical Pride Parade, complete with large puppets and banners trailing behind bicycles. An earnest Catholic priest at his information table encourages gays to come to his forward-looking, folksy services. Again I ponder if I might want to move here, in order to be able to continue working at Fort Lewis.

In one memorable client appointment, a middle-aged Black NCO seats himself on the office couch with a sigh, looking downcast. He came back a week earlier than expected from Iraq, having decided to surprise his wife. He heard rumors of her seeing another man, a married officer, and wanted to see for himself.

"She was so shocked when I showed up and confronted her.

She says they're just friends and it's purely *agape* love. Not sexual."

"Do you believe her?

"I don't know. We talked for two and a half hours. We've been together for seventeen years. Our son is sixteen." He's quiet for a moment, then continues, "I guess I was always like a drill sergeant at home, the big boss, you know. Now I wish I'd been able to be closer to them both. I hope there's something I can do. I don't want to lose my marriage."

We talk further and schedule a joint session, but first I want to see her alone. She comes in willingly, an attractive blonde white woman in neat, casual business clothes.

"He showed up without telling me he was coming home early. I wasn't prepared to talk with him yet. It's true I've been seeing a lot of this guy Doug and I'm starting to have some feelings for him, but we haven't done anything sexual."

I look at her with a question in my eyes.

"I wouldn't cheat on my husband. I'd say if I was. But I need some time to think. I've been angry with Randall for years for being so distant and controlling, but we have a child."

"Do you feel you still love him?"

"Oh, that's not it. Of course I love him, but I don't know if he'll really be able to change like he says he will."

I wait to see what else she might say. She starts to cry softly for a few moments, then says, "I might just be too mad to keep trying."

I let her sit with this a bit, then agree, "A lot to think about here. It may take a little time to sort out."

When they return together the following week, they are both smiling, but their laughter is nervous. Both are calm and poised, yet she especially seems tense, tightly-wrapped. He wants her to admit "wrongdoing" and she is not prepared to do so, feeling defensive.

"It's too soon for her to say what you want to hear," I tell him. "Give it some time. Pressure doesn't help."

"I know, I know. I've been praying on it. I care about her safety, her well-being. I know I've been controlling, and it's a habit that's hard to break."

"I feel he's always watching me now. I feel scrutinized. It's not comfortable. I do need some time to be alone but that makes him nervous."

Randall comes in for one more session, and that's the last I hear from either of them. It's my turn to pray on it, because there's nothing else I can do.

WHAT THIS WORK SHOWS ME is that military personnel and families are not different from other Americans, but their challenges are unique. Observing this at close range, I develop compassion for those who have agreed to carry arms and fight. Our democratically-elected civilian government makes the decisions about going to war, not the military, not the soldiers, sailors, airmen or marines. They feel that defending their country is an honorable profession despite the qualms they often share with civilians about whether the battles are well-chosen, appropriate, or justified. No one returns from deployment to a war zone unchanged, and the legacy of injury and trauma will be playing out in the lives of military members and their families and communities for years to come.

Friends write from time to time, asking about the news of suicide among soldiers. A half-dozen soldiers at Fort Lewis have killed themselves already this year, but it is not a topic of general conversation. The suicide rate among military personnel has slowly increased since the beginning of the Iraq and Afghanistan wars. Presumably this is one of the factors leading to the continued expansion of the Merk program. Big Army harrumphs a lot and talks tough about confronting this issue and making sure this selfish and misguided behavior stops. Big Army does not welcome a discussion on the impact of multiple deployments or the rates on PTSD.

The chaplains voice concern for the soldiers' souls. The Behavioral Health department produces poignant video training materials to raise awareness about depression and to encourage a helpful response in those around the soldiers. But at the day-to-day operational level in the squads and platoons, the reality is often much less compassionate. I can almost hear the sergeants saying, "This isn't group therapy. We're staying focused on getting tough for battle. Keep it simple: we're the good guys, and we're going to kill bad guys. We want to be heroes, not cowards. Get a grip, or get outta here." The causes of each suicide are multiple and complex, culture-driven and uniquely personal, and often hard to discern. They continue to happen, despite all the efforts at prevention.

I've been paying regular visits to an off-base GI coffee house, Coffee Strong, run by veterans of the wars the military has dubbed "Operation Iraqi Freedom" and "Operation Enduring Freedom." Located in a small shopping center in Lakewood just across the freeway from Fort Lewis, its aim is to provide a place for current soldiers to share their experiences, to air out their problems, to learn more about their rights, and to connect with the local anti-war organizations. Asked why he thinks soldiers are killing themselves at increasing rates, a volunteer staff member replies, "It's the multiple deployments. Not hard to figure this out." Then he tells me soldiers often joke, "If I'm going to kill myself, it will be when I'm sitting in one of those boring anti-suicide briefs."

In August, I attend the "State of the Soldier" forum at King's Books in Tacoma, where eye-opening stories are shared that are not told publicly on the base. A military widow talks about her husband's suicide two months ago. He was an Army Ranger (an elite corps) who had deployed eight times in eight years and had become a heavy drinker. She describes how he was poorly treated by the Rangers after his PTSD and suicidal thoughts became known.

Another speaker is a woman Marine who describes how her fellow Marine was raped and then killed herself. "There are two Marine Corps," she said. "The public one is upright and tries to appear perfect. The other is violent and brutal. But it's just a pressurized microcosm of civil society. This is the heart of darkness we all have." She has articulated the paradox that has troubled me all along. The military world is full of secrets, contradictions, pain, honor, joy, shame, and every other aspect of human experience. A simple description can never be given.

THE INTERPERSONAL DYNAMICS AMONG THE MERKS, whose number varies from six to eight, change over the year as people rotate in and out. Some are haughty or clueless, but now and then someone shows up whose company I enjoy. Mostly the work group is not a source of camaraderie or shared vision for me. But I've been amusing myself composing a talking "MRC Blues" and so when the group gets together for a party one night toward the end of this assignment, I take a risk and sing it for them. The song bemoans the stress of early-morning plane departures and the whiplash of being inserted and then withdrawn from different bases, and mocks our Malwell minders and the cloak-and-dagger atmosphere that's promoted by so much secrecy. I enjoy wailing out the chorus, "I've got the M-R-, M-R-, I've got the old M-R-C Blues!" The smiling and laughing shows me I can sometimes make a connection with this gang.

Increasingly, Merks are being asked to commit to six-month assignments, which would doubtless improve the effectiveness of the program. But that length of time away from home would be too long for me to tolerate. Though rotations are still three months at Fort Lewis, as a non-local I won't be able to return here. On the website where short-notice openings are posted, I find I can be paid to travel to Germany for three months during the least-desirable season, from mid-October to mid-January. People wanting to spend holidays with family would not want to choose such a timeframe, but I have no special plans. Now feeling fully recovered from the stress of the Korea assignment and actually ready for another challenge, I click the box and within days get a call from one of the mysterious assigners, saying a posting in Schweinfurt is available. Housing and a generous per diem are included, and shared use of a rental car. It will be a far cry from the Alpine beauty of Garmisch, but I accept it, relieved that at least for now, I will still have a source of income.

I ARRIVE BACK IN ASHLAND JUST IN TIME for a historic event: a Tibetan Buddhist teacher is in town for several days to bless and consecrate a new Tibetan-style temple funded by local Buddhists. This 21-year-old man is said to be the reincarnation of the revered Kalu Rinpoche, with whom my local American lamas have studied. Fluent in English, delightfully irreverent, he almost seems skeptical of his re-incarnated status. He probably scandalizes some in the crowd when he says, "Don't be so Tibetan!" He's also been asked to conduct a ceremony in which people take *bodhisattva* vows. I've heard of this for years and have been reading *The Way of the Bodhisattva* by Shantideva, but always felt that I wasn't ready to take a vow "to awaken all the beings of the world." Yet he's saying, in effect, that we are already on that path with our intention "to be good," and all we need to do is to love all beings as equal to ourselves. I'm not yet that open-hearted, but see no problem with having the intention and the aspiration to be so. I smile at the charming young man, join in the ceremony, and leave feeling entirely peaceful, hoping that the posting in Schweinfurt will be full of opportunities to practice.

Then another visit with Mom. Her mental acuity has steadily declined in the past few years, and it's painful to watch her mind disintegrate. Chunks simply fall off from time to time now. It's sobering to imagine that this could be me in twenty-five years. She's now moved to an assisted living facility in Camarillo, California in order to be closer to my younger sister. She's no longer the strong, controlling woman I had to fight with for my independence; instead she's increasingly anxious and dependent. She's so happy when we go out for a Whopper at Burger King, and delighted to get a cream-filled doughnut at her favorite shop in Port Hueneme. "I love you, Mommy," I say, more than I ever used to. Heading for Germany, I'm going to miss her ninetieth birthday. My tears start as I get into the car to leave. She smiles and gently waves as I drive away.

CHAPTER 15

BODHISATTVA RIDES AGAIN

2011-2012

No one is on the platform to greet me in Schweinfurt. A black compact car pulls over in the loading zone in front of the tiny station, and a nicely-dressed black woman rolls down the passenger window.

"Are you Maureen?" With that confirmed, she opens the trunk and helps me stow my luggage. "I'm Adrienne. I'm a Merk, too. I'll take you to get your documents." As she fastens her seatbelt she adds, "My sense of direction is really poor. I'll have to concentrate hard to find the way." She grips the steering wheel and looks around frantically before pulling out into traffic. She frowns and murmurs softly to herself as she scans the upcoming intersections, which precludes all but the most perfunctory conversation. I'm touched by the warm glow of amber autumn light falling on the rust-colored leaves still remaining in the trees as we pass. The dark time of the year has already begun, and the amount of daylight will be shrinking fast.

We stop to pick up my base pass, then drive through guarded

gates onto the grassy grounds of the Army base, stopping at an old two-story red brick building where a large wooden sign tells us we've arrived at the Bradley Inn.

"This is where all of us Merks are staying," says Adrienne. "You'll meet Susan later." After helping me get my luggage to my second-story room, she excuses herself and drives away.

The rooms at the Bradley Inn are large and high-ceilinged, with old furniture, worn carpets, and peeling paint. Internet connection is spotty, but there is a communal kitchen at the end of the hall. My room reeks of air freshener. When I open windows to air it out, the underlying smell of stale tobacco smoke ingrained in the carpets and furniture and even in the paint on the walls becomes obvious.

This German military base was taken over by Allied Forces at the end of World War II, and initially used as an air base and a camp for displaced European refugees. During the Cold War some 300,000 U.S. troops were stationed in Europe, with Schweinfurt among the larger sites. Since the collapse of the Soviet Union, the U.S. uses these bases as staging areas for deployments to wars in Iraq and Afghanistan, with soldiers and families typically stationed here for two to three-year assignments. For many years it was a thriving military community with its own schools and social activities, but recent drawdowns have left this base sparsely settled. Other garrisons have been completely closed and the land returned to the Germans.

My new coworkers seem withdrawn and minimally friendly. Adrienne, always stylishly-dressed and well-coiffed, plays her cards close to the chest, sharing little about herself. Susan, a petite white woman with short dark hair comes across as unsmiling and cranky.

"Do you believe it?" she says. "They assign three Merks and only give us two cars. It's insulting."

Two cars means we need to be regularly in touch to be sure we'll be able to get where we need to go. Because the base is in two sections several miles apart, walking everywhere is not an option. I start off being as happy and friendly as I know how to be, hoping to make some real human connection with my fellow Merks, but within a week or two I stop trying so hard and decide I'm on my own.

I'm attracted to Mona, the charismatic Hispanic woman who is our Army Community Services point of contact. She's always in fashion, wearing tight-fitting clothes that show off her figure, and I make an effort to guard my gaze. This is the first time I've had a POC who makes it her business to work with the commanders of every unit to understand the soldiers' issues and needs so that she can direct resources to serve them. Passionate about her work, she tries to inspire others to this level of caring. She gives us a lengthy briefing the first week, describing the various units we may be working with.

Half the 44th Signal Battalion is deployed to Afghanistan, and among those soldiers left behind in the rear detachment were some being discharged for bad behavior, some facing criminal charges, a few with unplanned pregnancies, plus one suicide.

Half the 172nd Support Battalion also did not deploy, leaving notable morale problems among those left behind in garrison who have little to do. They can be seen engaged in make-work projects such as raking leaves, probably wishing that instead they could have gone downrange.

Most of the 1st Battalion of the 77th Armor Regiment deployed to Iraq last year to provide security and assistance to

Iraqi forces. A Delta Company soldier was killed in June. Another soldier killed himself shortly after being reassigned to a U.S. base.

Thanks to Mona's efforts to publicize the presence of Merks, I see three or four clients each week for scheduled appointments. Yet we are directed by our bosses at Malwell to file activity reports to account for six to fourteen "direct contacts" every day, without fail. Coming in outside these specified parameters would be to court a reprimand or other unwanted attention from our overseers. Therefore, my reports include real or imaginary brief conversations, or even nods and smiles with various military-connected persons. I can't remember exactly when I gave up feeling guilty about using my imagination to fulfill this reporting expectation.

By the end of the week, I'm getting bummed by the aloofness of the Merks, the continued stink of my room, the lack of work to do, and the dimming of the daylight. Despite Mona's pep talks, I'm already counting the days until I can leave. It occurs to me that I am in a hotel room in a strange place where no one knows me, completely removed from friends and comfort — precisely the recommendation that Don Juan made in a book by Carlos Castaneda for a method of entirely "getting over yourself." I listen to a recording of the spiritual teacher Adyashanti on "The Dissolution of the Ego" and hear, "It's only the ego that suffers." That becomes a comforting reminder when I feel unhappy — not to identify with the emotional weather, not to jump on the thought-train of "ain't it awful?" that often chugs by.

Nevertheless, my moods go up and down, and I struggle to find ways to make myself useful and to pass the time. Mona has assigned me to be informally embedded with the 72nd Signal Battalion, which means we have the support of the commander. I am welcome to attend morning formation where all soldiers in the unit line up neatly in the yard next to the motor pool.

The First Sergeant takes attendance, and the Commander gives a quick briefing about the expectations for the coming days. On Fridays, the First Sergeant exhorts them not to do anything stupid over the weekend. By the time they get into this formation at 8 a.m., they've already had breakfast and done at least an hour of physical training. A couple of times each week, I show up dressed in my heaviest long underwear, warm slacks, heavy socks, a coat, gloves, and a warm hat. It's obvious who I am, the only one in civilian clothing. After this brief meeting, most of the soldiers go off to tinker with each company's vehicles in the motor pool bays. I wander about, struggling to engage some of them in small talk, but before long I'm headed for somewhere to warm up. Because of this special connection and the openness of the current commander, a colonel, I'm able to have good chats with him as well as his second-in-command, the XO, who is a major. Both have encouraged their soldiers to contact me for private sessions, but few actually do.

Given how rarely my business phone rings, I am delighted when a woman calls and asks to be seen with her husband. She arrives neatly dressed, with a head of shiny black curly hair, carrying a sleeping infant in a rocking carrier. Specialist Fortuna, a trim, good-looking man with an olive complexion, follows her into the room in his battle uniform. Settling themselves on a small tweed couch behind a coffee table, they look at each other and smile nervously. From my swivel chair opposite them, I first admire their sleeping child, and then ask what brings them here.

"We've been arguing a lot since the baby was born," she says. "I don't know why we do, but it's making me feel terrible. He's deploying to Iraq in two months, and I want us to get back to feeling close before he leaves."

She pauses, and I nod, waiting to see what else we will have to work with. I turn toward her husband to see if he has an opening statement, too.

"It's just really hard now with the baby," he says. "I wanted to wait until I was closer to completing my four years so we wouldn't have to deal with all this at once."

"But you were the one so keen on having a child! I wouldn't have minded waiting, too, but babies come when they do." She turns to me. "We were using birth control, but maybe we slipped a time or two, and I ended up pregnant. He was an angel during the pregnancy, but now he seems mad all the time."

"Is the baby disturbing your sleep?" I ask him.

"God, yes!" he exclaims, then admits, "She's the one who gets up with the baby, but I'm a light sleeper, and it's hard to go back to sleep."

She gives him a look, to which he responds, "I know, I know, it's hard for you too. But I have to get to work by 7:30 no matter what. It's hard without enough sleep."

They tell me the triggers for their arguments are many and often slight, but then minor differences escalate into conflict. I ask how angry they can get. Do they yell? Insult each other?

"He was never like this before. He doesn't exactly yell, but he says mean things."

"Well, you can be harsh, too. Really harsh."

During the brief silence following this interchange, I feel grateful that they made the effort to come in, and optimistic about their receptiveness to counseling because they arrived together and continue to speak of their feelings in an open manner.

Some of their distress seems a normal reaction to the sleeplessness and stress of having a new child, and they weren't expecting to be parents quite this soon. Asked what qualities they appreciated in their spouse that first drew them together, they are able to name some of them. At that point the tension starts to dissipate. He can't get time off next week, but they agree to an appointment the following week. I ask them to be mindful of the language they use with each other, and to try to cool the flames before arguments escalate. And the beautiful baby slept through it all.

BY THE END OF THE FIRST MONTH, I've discovered ways to amuse myself and keep my spirits up. A local folk/jazz club on the river near downtown advertises a klezmer concert. Two talented men who call their duo Nu play haunting music on accordion and clarinet. I understand only about one word in ten of their patter between numbers, but gather that though they are not Jewish, they have a deep love for this music. The audience of middle-aged Germans listens raptly, and shows its appreciation with energetic applause. I return to the club another night to hear a different folk duo, and this time the whole audience is so merry that they sing along in English on the chorus of Johnny Cash's "Ring of Fire." Though I know no one here, I feel I am among friends.

One sunny, frosty afternoon I come upon a low bunker-like structure on the base that is half-underground, with a small sign tacked to the building: "Arts and Crafts Center." Concrete steps descend to the basement level, where dangling fluorescent lights illuminate a series of long narrow rooms. Art supplies and partially-finished projects piled floor to ceiling are covered in a layer of fine dust. A woman with a soft face and long straight gray hair sits on a high stool by a workbench, writing in a small, worn notebook. She looks up, surprised. I introduce myself and invite her to tell me what goes on here.

"We have a lot of materials for the soldiers and families to use, as you can see. Ceramics, woodworking. Though not as many come as used to."

"You've worked here a long time?"

"Thirty years. My husband and I used to be paid, but then we retired and now we're volunteers, since there's hardly any budget anymore."

"Thirty years! You must have seen this base go through a lot of changes."

She smiles briefly and reflects, gazing into the distance. "Back in the eighties and nineties, we had a big German-American friendship club. But the Germans aren't so keen on this anymore, and soldiers don't show much interest either."

"But you must have made German friends yourself?"

"Some good friends, yes. Most Americans come and go, but we've made a home here. I think there's still a *Stammtisch* every month at a Greek restaurant, but we haven't been in a while."

"*Stammtisch*?"

"A regular table set aside for the club on the first Wednesday evening. Would you like to go sometime?"

"I'd love that."

Clara and her husband Max make a plan for us to meet at the restaurant the next first Wednesday, where I find them seated at a round table of polished dark wood in a dimly-lit, low-ceilinged room. We order our food and wait for others to come, but no one does.

"I guess we're the only ones tonight," says Max sheepishly. "Sorry to disappoint."

We enjoy our meal nonetheless, and they're happy to share anecdotes from the past, acknowledging that the vibrant era they recall has come to an end. Several years later, when I learn that the Schweinfurt base has been closed and the land returned to the Germans who use it as a camp for Syrian refugees, I wonder what became of Clara and Max.

Over the Veterans' Day holiday weekend, I take a solo train trip to Dresden, which for many years was in East Germany. I visit the newly re-opened military museum there, having read an interesting architectural magazine review. I also attend a symphony concert at the entirely rebuilt Frauenkirche which was bombed to rubble by the Allies at the end of World War II. Both visits are interesting but not enlivening, and the cold is bitter, with temperatures in the thirties.

A stranger agrees to take a photo of me at a stand-up table at a bar set up outside a department store near my hotel. My hands are wrapped around a mug of hot *Glühwein*, a traditional German Christmas drink. The midnight-blue mug is decorated with a winter scene and the words, "Dresdener Weinachtsmarkt." I look bulky wearing long underwear, and two sweaters under my gray outer jacket. A corduroy cap on my head does not look as jaunty as I had hoped it might. I smile tensely into the camera, trying to imagine I am having a good time.

Locals in stylish, black, close-fitting clothes surround me at tables as outdoor heaters struggle to dispel the cold. Strings of small white lights illuminate the area with a soft sparkle. The air is tinged with the smell of cinnamon and hot pastry. Swallowing the hot spicy wine, I feel my tongue curl and my chest warm from the inside. I am searching for the courage to approach a table of strangers in order to make human contact. I cannot think of what to say in my halting German, so I remain stiffly alone.

The sound of live singing drifts to my ears, and I follow the music around the corner of the building. A middle-aged man with a grizzled beard sits on a stool, playing guitar and singing folk music from the 1960s. He's wearing fingerless gloves and his guitar case is open for donations. His singing Bob Dylan in a husky baritone voice moves me with a sense of fellow-feeling for this solitary soul. But then it's so cold that I retreat to the bar and stand under an outdoor heater, studying the drinks menu. I order another mug of *Glühwein*, this time fortified with a shot of spirits. On an impulse, I say, "Make that two!" and return to where the man is singing. He smiles and accepts the drink I hand him As the liquor takes effect and I sway gently to the music, I know this is the closest I'll feel to anyone on this winter's night.

After returning from Dresden, I'm asked to prepare a presentation on "Staying Positive in Negative Situations." The hours it takes to gather my thoughts is a good exercise for me. I'll include a lot about self-care, and the importance of being flexible, not rigid, so we can handle whatever comes at us. After writing an outline and practicing my delivery, I go to the designated meeting room and no one shows up. This is a pattern I've grown used to, and the disappointment offers another opportunity to practice what I was about to preach.

The weather gets darker and colder. The sun comes up at 8 a.m., cruises sideways along the horizon, briefly reaches a point 40 degrees above the horizon by midday, then starts going down and is completely gone by 4 p.m. I buy a couple of cooking pots to use in the ill-equipped communal kitchen, and start making myself hearty winter soups. I discover the gorgeous public swimming hall in Schweinfurt, with an indoor Olympic-size pool, an outdoor steaming warm pool, a cold dip, a sauna, and even a rope attached to an overhead bucket of ice, which can be pulled after getting out of the hot sauna, to dump ice on your head. The alternation between hot and cold experiences reliably reduces me to a puddle of warm, relaxed protoplasm. I go there a couple of evenings each week.

A half-hour drive takes me to the small town of Bad Kissingen, where natural mineral springs feed the luxurious yet affordable Kissalis spa. Besides hot pools, steam rooms, and a swimming area, there is a set of cedar huts containing saunas of varying temperatures, surrounding a lighted cold pool glowing turquoise in the night. How much more comfortable Europeans are with nudity compared with Americans! In the unclad sauna area, I occasionally see whole families with children eight to ten years old, ambling about peacefully. One night I get so hot and happy and relaxed in the sauna that I look around and feel a surge of love for these naked strangers, these men and women, these beautiful human beings. I have that feeling of, "We're all in this together" that comes over me, only too rarely.

During our conference call the Wednesday before Thanksgiving, Ralph the supervisor oozes, "I want to personally thank each and every one of you for the sacrifices you make to be here for the troops in the holiday season." He then informs us the word "challenges" that we'd been taught to substitute in our reports for "problems," is no longer the word of choice. We are instead to refer now only to "opportunities." Gag.

On Thanksgiving, both dining facilities offer a big feast, which includes a roast pig. Perhaps it's a nod to the *Schwein* in Schweinfurt. The food is otherwise the same unremarkable cafeteria food they usually serve, but there is plenty of it, and by custom, the officers put on aprons and serve the food. Some families attend, but mostly it's single soldiers who don't have other plans. I eat with Adrienne, Susan, and the Merks who work with children, and afterward we drive downtown to the outdoor Christmas Market in the central square.

Schweinfurt is a small industrial town of about 50,000, and definitely not a tourist destination. The market is modest: a few booths with drinks and cookies and some gift items. We have a glass of holiday spiced wine, but we're not dressed warmly enough for the intensity of the cold, so we soon head back to base.

That weekend I dress in my warmest clothes and pile into a car with Merks from the children's program for a trip to Rothenburg, a medieval walled city about an hour away. We arrive late in the day because we want to stay for the Night Watchman Tour which starts at 8 p.m. I leave the group at the large and colorful central Christmas Market and enjoy a solitary walk about the ramparts of the city in the slanting late afternoon light. Looking out on the rolling hills of the countryside, I try to imagine myself living here in the 13th century.

We have sausages for dinner, and listen to an organ concert in historic St. Jakob's Church. Then we meet up with the Night Watchman, a tall bearded man clad in a heavy black cape with a hood. He carries a halberd (a long pike with an axe blade) and a lantern. Despite his ominous appearance, he easily engages the group, speaking excellent English. He escorts us around the oldest area of the city, the click of his boot heels echoing off the stone paths. We learn the story of the night watchman's job, as well as the history of the ancient buildings, illuminated at night. The excitement and mystery grow as snow starts to fall, and again I imagine we have moved back in time.

In these weeks, I'm taking a distance-learning class with my Ashland Buddhist lamas, called "Heroic Awakening." We're using Pema Chodron's book *No Time to Lose* to study the eighth-century Indian sage Shantideva's text, *The Way of the Bodhisattva*. I've drifted from thinking about the *bodhisattva* vows I took before coming here, and admonish myself to meditate more regularly. I wish to increase my acceptance of the world as it is, and to keep my heart open as much as I am able.

While spending an evening reading Buddhist books and listening to lectures, a spouse calls me for an appointment. I welcome the opportunity to serve. She's grieving the death of her stillborn baby four months ago. The many self-help methods she's tried to contend with her feelings have not worked, and she is becoming increasingly anxious and depressed, concerned that her mental state is not good for her other two children.

"I need my husband," she says. "He's got to come home from downrange to help me."

At the Behavioral Health clinic she was told they had no openings for six weeks. The chaplain could recommend the soldier be granted emergency leave, but her husband's unit chaplain is out of town. I help her get in touch with her husband's commander and encourage her to go back to Behavioral Health and emphasize that she is truly in crisis. Her OB/GYN provider may also have some suggestions on postpartum depression. We do some relaxation and breathing techniques, and I offer to meet with her for support until she can get connected with the right people.

On December 9 at 9 p.m. I drive to the closed Recreation Center and sit outside in the parking lot. Here is where I can get a strong enough wi-fi signal to complete a Skype call to California. It's my mother's ninetieth birthday, and my relatives are gathered at my younger sister's house. Balancing my laptop against the steering wheel, I'm able to see a fuzzy rendition of all their faces, one by one. Mom is bewildered by the technology but seems pleased at their efforts to include me. We sing an out-of-synch version of Happy Birthday, and we all wave to each other. That's the limit of what we can do on this long-distance connection tonight. I don't think anyone can see the tears in my eyes.

STILL STRUGGLING TO FIND ENOUGH WORK TO DO, I'm shocked to learn that Mona believes this base could use even more Merks. I guess she has been provided those phony statistics about how busy we are. Now she has made a formal request to Malwell for two additional coaches. Perhaps she imagines if we have enough people in place, the clients will come. So just as I put dour Susan and remote Adrienne on the train and wish them farewell, four new Merks arrive to replace them.

Now that we will be sharing three cars among five people, it gets complicated. Everyone wants their own car, and tries to justify it.

"I'm going to work with the 12th Chemical Company," says Fred, a fifty-something man with pimples and a paunch. "They have workspace on both campuses of the base, and I'll need a car to drive back and forth."

"I absolutely must swim every day," insists Alice, a thin muscular woman who looks anorexic. "My health depends on it. I can't be worrying about getting a ride to the pool from someone else."

"My mother is very ill. She lives in France," says Arnold, who wears his hair slicked back in a style reminiscent of Italian gangsters. "I'm in touch with her every day and I have to be able to get to a spot on the base with strong wi-fi so I can use Skype. Without a car, I might not be able to reach her when she needs me."

"I've always had my own car on other assignments," whines Terrence, a lanky man younger than the rest of us. "I don't know how we can be expected to show up to appointments if we don't have reliable transportation."

Impressed with their lack of cooperative spirit, I smile inwardly. Really, people? No one shows a desire to cooperate or be creative in finding a solution. As the de facto leader of this misbegotten group, I volunteer to draw up a schedule and present it to them the next day. Each will have primary access to a car three days a week and make other arrangements on the other days. They accept this grudgingly.

Then I learn that the new foursome has hatched a plan to fly to Barcelona for the three-day Christmas weekend. Disregarding our instructions not to ask for extra time off on Fridays, and unconcerned about how it may reflect on their commitment to the job, they tell Mona the POC that they want flex time to extend the holiday to four days. She doesn't try to stop them. I say I'll hold down the fort since I don't mind just staying indoors and cooking oxtail stew in my room, reading books and watching DVDs from the base library. I'm relieved when they clear out and I have all three cars to myself.

It's deep winter, now. We've not had a lot of snow yet, but it's cold and dark — definitely a good time to draw inward. I'm still reading *The Way of the Bodhisattva*, whose inspiring set of writings in verse explain the importance of compassion and committing oneself to helping others. To be more loving, like a *bodhisattva*, like Jesus, is an aspiration I've had all my life, though my progress has been slow.

When I meet with clients, compassion naturally arises as they confide their troubles and I give them my full attention. Then I'm on the *bodhisattva* path. I get frustrated though, when I'm idle, and I've been idle much of the time I've been paid to work in these military settings over the years. I've questioned the absurdity of the situation many times. In this calm and quiet midwinter, I'm able to ask the question that's been haunting me: Why am I doing this?

More and more, I've been unhappy playing this game, pretending to have a job helping others while the real reason I'm here is to pay my bills. Then I reflect that after five years taking these contracts I actually have paid off my bills, and perhaps I could let go of this morally-questionable dissembling and find more satisfying work.

Assignments at Fort Lewis have receded from my grasp, so all I can look forward to is further overseas rotations, which increasingly are for three or even six months. I am tired of the loneliness, and I've been feeling my age more. Each trip through airport security is a further erosion of dignity. Soon, I think it will be time to unpack my bags, relax and write my book.

But what a ride it's been. From darkest Kentucky to windswept Colorado, from the forests of the Pacific Northwest to the fields of Gettysburg, I've been able to use my time to grow in knowledge and wisdom about the functioning of the military establishment and aid in the challenges of the people who work within it. With my journal, my laptop and a camera as companions, I've been able to maintain my sanity and keep in touch with friends at home. I could probably snag a few more overseas trips and a few more dollars, but I think I've learned what I can from these experiences. It's time to stand down, as they say in the military — time to retire from the field of battle.

A GREAT MANY OF THE SOLDIERS have left the Schweinfurt base for holiday leave, so there is no work to do. On a quiet Christmas morning in a sort of reverie, I write a lengthy letter to myself in my journal. I express gratitude to the part of myself that comforts me when I'm blue, that encourages me when I'm fearful, and that regards me with love and acceptance. It's odd to speak of this inner dialogue, but I'm glad to recognize that I'm not actually alone. I can feel accompanied by a loving presence that is available for comfort and guidance. This insight helps me remain peaceful in trying circumstances.

I have a final session with the sweet couple who I've been counseling for two months. They thank me for helping them stabilize their new relationship and stop fighting over whose idea it was to have their adorable baby. At formation one morning, the colonel presents me with a framed certificate of appreciation from the 72nd Signal Battalion for my time with them. I agree to go out to a country inn for a family-style farewell dinner with all the other Merks. I've come to see the pathos in their selfish behavior and accept that they are this way. I'm amused that they now seem to defer to me and express gratitude that I joined them for dinner.

On New Year's Eve, I'm in the kitchen of the Bradley Inn making another delicious chicken soup, and as often happens, I'm joined by someone else cooking their dinner. This time it is a young, newly-minted officer in the Army National Guard, here with his wife who is regular Army. They met in officer training school and she was just sent here to join the 12th Chemical Battalion. He'll live with her in Germany and fly back to the States once a month to train with his Guard unit. He chose National Guard because it enabled him to pick his specialty, armored cavalry, and now he is maneuvering to switch to regular Army.

"I'm going over to their office to kiss some major butt with the colonel next week," he says, hoping that there will be an opening for him.

I am touched by his excitement over joining a unit of paratroopers who have been doing reconnaissance in remote areas of Afghanistan, and impressed with the physical courage and dedication required of these soldiers. He's curious about me, too, and asks how I got involved in what he terms "Army social work."

This is always hard for me to explain. I can't just tell him that it pays well, I learn a lot, and I'm planning to write a book. Though not a natural ally of the armed services, I have come to respect and care about the people who bravely put their lives on the line wherever their country sends them to fight, and I hope something of that feeling comes across to him. I don't even try to explain how I've also been in training to be a *bodhisattva*.

2013

The waves slap the seawall as night falls on Izmir Bay, and the call to prayer resounds over the city. The men selling fresh oysters and roasted corn are packing up their hand trucks. Families shake out picnic blankets and stroll away along the Kordon walkway.

Further down the coast in Çeşme, a woman swims alone on a private beach by the Aegean Sea, marveling at the good fortune that has brought her to this land of kind people and intriguing culture. After a buffet dinner of Turkish delicacies served at the hotel, she takes a glass of anise-flavored *raki* mixed with water, and finds a seat outside on a wide deck under the full moon, completely alone, entirely peaceful. She tries to memorize this moment of freedom and relaxation as her final assignment with the military comes to a close.

Despite her plan to quit this work, she just cannot refuse when offered a posting in Turkey for three months. Sent to work in both Izmir and Ankara with a handful of Air Force personnel who were entirely squared away with no desire for counseling, she dives into the base library's collection of Turkish history and literature and follows Turkish politics via CNN, Al-Jazeera, and an English-language newspaper. Weekends are free to explore this ancient land where Greeks once settled in seaside fishing communities, with agrarian and nomadic speakers of other tongues in the interior.

Empires rose and fell, ruins of citadels abound, Christian monks hid underground for years in desert caves, dervishes whirled, and Rumi wrote poetry in Konya. Even having no work to do, no standing, and no peers, she resolves to enjoy it all: the luxury of the Hilton hotel, the cacophony of the bazaar, the vibrant beauty of hand-woven carpets, and the turquoise Aegean Sea.

In Ankara, she meets with the Turkish man she found in an online search, who wants to translate Buddhist writings into Turkish. He has made pilgrimages to Daramsala to visit the Dalai Lama, and like the Dalai Lama, is both jolly and wise. They meet to talk for the first time in Kugulu Park, watching the swans glide over the pond. Trampled grass and red graffiti on walls remain from a rare anti-government demonstration that week. He deflects a political question, saying, "I try to look at things nakedly, just as they are, and not get caught in judgment. It doesn't work to criticize ourselves or make a problem of what *is.*" With a mischievous chuckle he adds, "Resistance is futile!" His warmth is a balm for her loneliness. When they dine with his girlfriend at a local restaurant, he speaks to the chef who later brings out a three-foot loaf of bread with *Buddhadharma* (the teachings of the Buddha) spelled out in poppy seeds. A perfect statement of the nourishment the teachings offer to people of all cultures.

When she later remembers that scene in the park, it is as though her new friend is glowing, almost floating above that grimy city, the defaced park, the nervous angry people. But at the time, all she'd noticed was that in his presence her spirit grew quieter. She dares not write to him now, fearing communication with a foreigner might cause him trouble. Instead, she remembers him by praying:

"May you be safe. May you be happy.
May you be free.
May the people of Turkey be safe. May they be happy.
May they be free.
May all beings be safe. May all beings be happy.
May all beings be free."

And then she ends by offering this same prayer for herself.

ACKNOWLEDGMENTS

First I have to thank those pesky friends who were always telling me I needed to write a book. During my travels, I sent emails every two to three weeks to a group of friends and family, detailing what I was seeing and feeling in my encounters with the military. Their understanding responses held me up and carried me through difficult times. Their heartfelt replies gave me faith that I did belong to a community of caring, like-minded people, even though we were not within hugging distance. And their faith in me as a writer gave me the chutzpah to think I could actually do it — write a book.

I thank the Threshold Singers, who sing for people in the dying process, for welcoming me to join rehearsals between assignments, and for singing me blessings when I departed again. The members of a weekly free-writing group I attended for years were also instrumental in helping me find my voice.

Many thanks to my gentle lamas Pema and Yeshe, who helped me learn almost everything I know about Buddhism through their teaching and their example. Facilitating distance learning was a huge gift, as it gave me a valuable frame of reference as I interacted with the military.

During the years of writing, my buddies Connie and Elizabeth met with me every few weeks to share the latest chapters of our memoirs. Their feedback greatly improved my writing. Molly

Tinsley, editor and writing teacher, generously gave much of her time to revise and shape the book.

While completing the book this year, my Friday morning memoir class has been a source of joy and support. My coach and editor Ron Seybold has been invaluable in helping me, a digital tourist, find my way through the complexities of self-publishing with advice and good cheer. And my designer Asya Blue has wrapped the book in its beautiful cover.

But I can't begin to speak my gratitude for the love and support of my partner Keziah, whose insightful ideas and willingness to give me room allowed all this to happen, all the while being the best of company.

ABOUT THE AUTHOR

MAUREEN HICKS, PH.D. worked as a psychotherapist for thirty years in public and private mental health settings. She now lives with her partner in Olympia, Washington, where she enjoys choral singing and participates in a Buddhist meditation group.

Made in the USA
Middletown, DE
13 December 2023

45627076R00139